BELINDA

AN APRIL FOLLY IN THREE ACTS

A. A. MILNE

TRUE SIGN
PUBLISHING HOUSE

Published by True Sign Publishing House
Address: SY. No. 21/2 & 21/3, Sonnenahalli,
Krishnarajapura, Bengaluru,
Karnataka - 560049 India
E-mail: truesignbooks@gmail.com
Website: www.truesign.in

Belinda
An April Folly In Three Acts

Author: A. A. Milne

ISBN: 978-93-5584-198-8

First Edition: 2023

CONTENTS

Characters

Produced by Mr. Dion Boucioault at the New Theatre, London, on April 8, 1918, with the following cast:—

BELINDA TREMAYNE   -   Irene Vanbrugh.

DELIA (her Daughter)   -   Isabel Elsom.

HAROLD BAXTER   -   Dion Boucicault.

CLAUDE DEVENISH   -   Dennis Neilson-Terry.

JOHN TREMAYNE   -   Ben Webster.

BETTY   -   Anne Walden.

The action takes place in Belinda's country-house in Devonshire at the end of April, the first act in the garden and the second and last acts in the hall

Act - I

It is a lovely April afternoon–a foretaste of summer–in BELINDA'S garden. BETTY, a middle-aged servant, is fastening a hammock–its first appearance this year–to a tree down L. In front there is a garden-table, with a deck-chair on the right of it and a straight-backed one to the left. There are books, papers, and magazines on the table. BELINDA, of whom we shall know more presently, is on the other side of the open windows which look on to the garden, talking to BETTY, who crosses to R. of hammock, securing it to tree C.

BELINDA (from inside the house). Are you sure you're tying it up tightly enough, Betty?

BETTY (coming to front of hammock). Yes, ma'am; I think it's firm.

BELINDA. Because I'm not the fairy I used to be.

BETTY (testing hammock). Yes, ma'am; it's quite firm this end too.

BELINDA (entering from portico with sunshade open). It's not the ends I'm frightened of; it's the middle where the weight's coming. (Comes down R. and admiring.) It looks very nice. (She crosses at back of wicker table, hanging her hand-bag on hammock. Closes and places her sunshade at back of tree C.)

BETTY. Yes, ma'am.

BELINDA (trying the middle of it with her hand). I asked them at the Stores if they were quite sure it would bear me, and they said it would take anything up to–I forget how many tons. I know I thought it was rather rude of them. (Looking at it anxiously, and trying to get in, first with her right leg and then her left.) How does one get in! So trying to be a sailor!

BETTY. I think you sit in it, ma'am, and then (explaining with her hands) throw your legs over.

BELINDA. I see. (She sits gingerly in the hammock, and then, with a sudden flutter of white, does what BETTY suggests.) Yes. (Regretfully.) I'm afraid that was rather wasted on you, Betty. We must have some spectators next time.

BETTY. Yea, ma'am

BELINDA. Cushions.

(BETTY moves to and takes a cushion from deck-chair. BELINDA assists her to place it at back of her head. BETTY then goes to back of hammock and arranges BELINDA'S dress.)

There! Now then, Betty, about callers.

BETTY. Yes, ma'am.

BELINDA. If Mr. Baxter calls–he is the rather prim gentleman—

BETTY. Yea, ma'am; the one who's been here several times before. (Moves to below and L. of hammock.)

BELINDA (giving BETTY a quick look). Yes. Well, if he calls, you'll say, "Not at home."

BETTY. Yes, ma'am.

BELINDA. He will say (imitating MR. BAXTER), "Oh–er–oh–er–really." Then you'll smile very sweetly and say, "I beg your pardon, was it Mr. Baxter?" And he'll say, "Yes!" and you'll say, "Oh, I beg your pardon, sir; this way, please."

BETTY. Yes, ma'am.

BELINDA. That's right, Betty. Well now, if Mr. Devenish calls–he is the rather poetical gentleman—

BETTY. Yes, ma'am; the one who's always coming here.

BELINDA (with a pleased smile). Yes. Well, if he calls you'll say, "Not at home."

BETTY. Yes, ma'am.

BELINDA. He'll immediately (extending her arms descriptively) throw down his bunch of flowers and dive despairingly into the moat. You'll stop him, just as he is going in, and say, "I beg your pardon, sir, was it Mr. Devenish?" And he will say, "Yes!" and you will say, "Oh, I beg your pardon, sir; this way, please."

BETTY. Yes, ma'am. And suppose they both call together?

BELINDA (non-plussed for a moment). We won't suppose anything so exciting, Betty.

BETTY. No, ma'am. And suppose any other gentleman calls?

BELINDA (with a sigh). There aren't any other gentlemen.

BETTY. It might be a clergyman, come to ask for a subscription like.

BELINDA. If it's a clergyman, Betty, I shall–I shall want your assistance out of the hammock first.

BETTY. Yes, ma'am.

BELINDA. That's all.

(BETTY crosses below table and chairs to porch.)

To anybody else I'm not at home, (Trying to secure book on table and nearly falling out of the hammock.) Oh, just give me that little green book. (Pointing to books on the table.) The one at the bottom there–that's the one. (BETTY gives it to her.) Thank you. (Reading the title.) "The Lute of Love," by Claude Devenish. (To herself as she turns the pages.) It doesn't seem much for half-a-crown when you think of the Daily Telegraph .... Lute ... Lute .... I should have quite a pretty mouth if I kept on saying that. (With a great deal of expression.) Lute! (She pats her mouth back.)

BETTY. Is that all, ma'am?

BELINDA. That's all. (BETTY prepares to go.) Oh, what am I thinking of! (Waving to the table.) I want that review; I think it's the blue one. (As BETTY begins to look.) It has an article by Mr. Baxter on the "Rise of Lunacy in the Eastern Counties"—

(BETTY gives her "The Nineteenth Century" Magazine.)

–yes, that's the one. I'd better have that too; I'm just at the most exciting place. You shall have it after me, Betty.

BETTY. Is that all, ma'am?

BELINDA. Yes, that really is all.

(BETTY goes into the house.)

BELINDA (reading to herself very pronouncedly). "It is a matter of grave concern to all serious students of social problems–" (Putting the review down in hammock and shaking her head gently.) But not in April. (Lazily opening the book and reading.) "Tell me where is love"–well, that's the question, isn't it? (She lies back in the hammock lazily and the book of poems falls from her to the ground. DELIA comes into the garden, from Paris. She is decidedly a modern girl, pretty and self-possessed. Her hair is half-way up; waiting for her birthday, perhaps. She sees her mother suddenly, stops, and then goes on tiptoe to the head of the hammock. She smiles and kisses her mother on the forehead. BELINDA, looking supremely unconscious, goes on sleeping. DELIA kisses her lightly again. BELINDA wakes up with an extraordinarily natural start, and is just about to say, "Oh, Mr. Devenish–you mustn't!"–when she sees DELIA.) Delia! (They kiss each other frantically.)

DELIA. Well, mummy, aren't you glad to see me?

BELINDA. My darling child!

DELIA. Say you're glad.

BELINDA (sitting up). My darling, I'm absolutely–(DELIA crosses round to L. of hammock.) Hold the hammock while I get out, dear; we don't want an accident. (DELIA holds the L. end of it and BELINDA struggles out, leaving the magazine and her handkerchief in the hammock.) They're all right when you're there, and they'll bear two tons, but they're horrid getting in and out of. (Kissing her again.) Darling, it really is you?

DELIA. Oh, it is jolly seeing you again. I believe you were asleep.

BELINDA (with dignity). Certainly not, child. I was reading The Nineteenth Century–(with an air)–and after. (Earnestly) Darling, wasn't it next Thursday you were coming back?

DELIA. No, this Thursday, silly.

BELINDA (penitently). Oh, my darling, and I was going over to Paris to bring you home.

DELIA. I half expected you.

BELINDA. So confusing their both being called Thursday. And you were leaving school for the very last time. If you don't forgive me, Delia, I shall cry.

DELIA (kissing her and stroking her hand fondly). Silly mother!

(BELINDA sits down in the deck-chair and DELIA sits on the table.)

BELINDA. Isn't it a lovely day for April, darling! I've wanted to say that to somebody all day, and you're the first person who's given me the chance. Oh, I said it to Betty, but she only said, "Yes, ma'am."

DELIA. Poor mother!

BELINDA (jumping up suddenly, crossing to L. of and kissing DELIA again). I simply must have another one. And to think that you're never going back to school any more. (Looking at her fondly, and backing to L.) Darling, you are looking pretty.

DELIA. Am I?

BELINDA. Lovely. (She kisses her once more, then she takes the cushion from the hammock, moves at back of table and places it on the head of the deck-chair.) And now you're going to stay with me for just as long as you want a mother. (Anxiously moving to R. of deckchair.) Darling, you didn't mind being sent away to school, did you? It is the usual thing, you know.

DELIA. Silly mother! of course it is.

BELINDA (relieved, and sitting on deck-chair). I'm so glad you think so too.

DELIA. Have you been very lonely without me?

BELINDA (with a sly look at DELIA). Very.

DELIA (turning to BELINDA and holding up a finger). The truth, mummy!

BELINDA. I've missed you horribly, Delia. (Primly.) The absence of female companionship of the requisite—

DELIA. Are you really all alone?

BELINDA (smiling mysteriously and coyly). Well, not always, of course.

DELIA (excitedly, at she slips off the table, and backing to L. a little). Mummy, I believe you're being bad again.

BELINDA. Really, darling, you forget that I'm old enough to be–in fact, am–your mother.

DELIA (nodding her head). You are being bad.

BELINDA (rising with dignity and drawing herself up to her full height, moving L.). My child, that is not the way to–Oh, I say, what a lot taller I am than you! (Turning her back to DELIA and comparing sizes.)

DELIA. And prettier.

BELINDA (playfully rubbing noses with DELIA). Oh, do you think so? (Firmly, but pleased.) Don't be silly, child.

DELIA (holding up a finger). Now tell me all that's been happening here at once.

BELINDA (with a sigh). And I was just going to ask you how you were getting on with your French. (Sits in deck-chair.)

DELIA. Bother French! You've been having a much more interesting time than I have, so you've got to tell.

BELINDA (with a happy sigh). O-oh! (She sinks back into her chair.)

DELIA (taking off her coat). Is it like the Count at Scarborough?

BELINDA (surprised and pained). My darling, what do you mean?

DELIA. Don't you remember the Count who kept proposing to you at Scarborough? I do. (Places coat on hammock.)

BELINDA (reproachfully). Dear one, you were the merest child, paddling about on the beach and digging castles.

DELIA (smiling to herself). I was old enough to notice the Count.

BELINDA (sadly). And I'd bought her a perfectly new spade! How one deceives oneself!

DELIA (at table and leaning across, with hands on table). And then there was the M.P. who proposed at Windermere.

BELINDA. Yes, dear, but it wasn't seconded–I mean he never got very far with it.

DELIA. And the artist in Wales.

BELINDA. Darling child, what a memory you have. No wonder your teachers are pleased with you.

DELIA (settling herself comfortably in deck-chair L. of BELINDA and lying in her arms). Now tell me all about this one.

BELINDA (meekly). Which one?

DELIA (excitedly). Oh, are there lots?

BELINDA (severely). Only two.

DELIA. Two! You abandoned woman!

BELINDA. It's something in the air, darling. I've never been in Devonshire in April before.

DELIA. Is it really serious this time?

BELINDA (pained). I wish you wouldn't say this time, Delia. It sounds so unromantic. If you'd only put it into French–cette fois–it sounds so much better. Cette fois. (Parentally.) When one's daughter has just returned from an expensive schooling in Paris, one likes to feel—

DELIA. What I meant, dear, was, am I to have a stepfather at last?

BELINDA. Now you're being too French, darling.

DELIA. Why, do you still think father may be alive?

BELINDA. Why not? It's only eighteen years since he left us, and he was quite a young man then.

DELIA. Yes, but surely, surely you'd have heard from him in all those years, if he'd been alive?

BELINDA. Well, he hasn't heard from me, and I'm still alive.

DELIA (looking earnestly at her mother, rises and moves L.C.). I shall never understand it.

BELINDA. Understand what?

DELIA. Were you as heavenly when you were young as you are now?

BELINDA (rapturously). Oh, I was sweet!

DELIA. And yet he left you after only six months.

BELINDA (rather crossly, sitting up). I wish you wouldn't keep on saying he left me. I left him too.

DELIA (running to and kneeling in front of BELINDA and looking anxiously into her face). Why?

BELINDA (smiling to herself). Well, you see, he was quite certain he knew how to manage women, and I was quite certain I knew how to manage men. (Thoughtfully.) If only one of us had been certain, it would have been all right.

DELIA (seriously). What really happened, mummy? I'm grown up now, so I think you ought to tell me.

BELINDA (thoughtfully). That was about all, you know ... except for his beard.

DELIA. Had he a beard? (Laughing.) How funny!

BELINDA (roaring with laughter, in which DELIA joins). Yes, dear, it was; but he never would see it. He took it quite seriously.

DELIA. And did you say dramatically, "If you really loved me, you'd take it off"?

BELINDA (apologetically). I'm afraid I did, darling.

DELIA. And what did he say?

BELINDA. He said–very rudely–that, if I loved him, I'd do my hair in a different way.

DELIA (sinks down on her haunches, facing the audience). How ridiculous!

BELINDA (touching her hair). Of course, I didn't do it like this then. I suppose we never ought to have married, really.

DELIA. Why did you?

BELINDA. Mother rather wanted it. (Solemnly.) Delia, never get married because your mother— Oh, I forgot; I'm your mother.

DELIA. And I don't want a better one ... (They embrace.) And so you left each other?

BELINDA. Yes.

DELIA. But, darling, didn't you tell him there was going to be a Me?

BELINDA. Oh no!

DELIA. I wonder why not?

BELINDA. Well, you see, if I had, he might have wanted to stay.

DELIA. But—

BELINDA (hurt). If he didn't want to stay for me, I didn't want him to stay for you. (Penitently.) Forgive me, darling, but I didn't know you very well then. We've been very happy together, haven't we?

DELIA (going to the hammock, sitting in it and dangling her legs). I should think we have.

BELINDA (leaning back in chair). I don't want to deny you anything, and, of course, if you'd like a stepfather (looking down modestly) or two—

DELIA. Oh, you have been enjoying yourself.

BELINDA. Only you see how awkward it would be if Jack turned up in the middle of the wedding, like–like Eugene Aram.

DELIA. Enoch Arden, darling.

BELINDA. It's very confusing their having the same initials. Perhaps I'd better call them both E. A. in future and then I shall be safe. Well, anyhow it would be awkward, darling, wouldn't it? Not that I should know him from Adam after all these years–except for a mole on his left arm.

DELIA. Perhaps Adam had a mole.

BELINDA. No, darling; you're thinking of Noah. He had two.

DELIA (thoughtfully). I wonder what would happen if you met somebody whom you really did fall in love with?

BELINDA (reproachfully). Now you're being serious, and it's April.

DELIA. Aren't these two–the present two–serious?

BELINDA. Oh no! They think they are, but they aren't a bit, really. Besides, I'm doing them such a lot of good. I'm sure they'd hate to marry me, but they love to think they're in love with me, and–I love it, and–and they love it, and–and we all love it.

DELIA (rising and crossing to BELINDA). You really are the biggest, darlingest baby who ever lived. (Kisses her.) Do say I shan't spoil your lovely times.

BELINDA (surprised). Spoil them? Why, you'll make them more lovely than ever.

DELIA (turning away and sitting on table). Well, but do they know you have a grown-up daughter?

BELINDA (suddenly realizing and sitting up). Oh!

DELIA. It doesn't really matter, because you don't look a day more than thirty.

BELINDA (absently). No. (Hurriedly.) I mean, how sweet of you–only—

DELIA. What!

BELINDA (playing with her rings). Well, one of them, Mr. Baxter–Harold– (she looks quickly up at DELIA and down again in pretty affectation, but she is really laughing at herself all the time) he writes statistical articles for the Reviews–percentages and all those things. He's just the sort of man, if he knew that I was your mother, to work it out that I was more than thirty. The other one, Mr. Devenish–Claude–(she looks up and down as before) he's rather, rather poetical. He thinks I came straight from heaven–last week.

DELIA (laughing and jumping up and crossing below deck-chair to R. towards house). I think I'd better go straight back to Paris.

BELINDA (jumping up and catching her firmly by the left arm). You will do nothing of the sort. (Pulling DELIA back to centre.) You will take off

     BELINDA AN APRIL FOLLY IN THREE ACTS

that hat–(she lets go of the arm and begins to take out the pin) which is a perfect duck, and I don't know why I didn't say so before–(she puts the hat down on the table) and let me take a good look at you (she does so), and kiss you (she does so, then crosses DELIA below her and takes her towards the house), and then we'll go to your room and unpack and have a lovely talk about clothes. And then we'll have tea.

(BETTY comes in and stands up at back.)

And now here's Betty coming in to upset all our delightful plans, just when we've made them. (BELINDA and DELIA are now on BETTY'S R.)

DELIA (leaving BELINDA and shaking hands with BETTY). How are you, Betty? I've left school.

BETTY. Very nicely, thank you, miss. (Backing to L. and admiring.) You've grown.

BELINDA (moving to and patting the top of DELIA'S head). I'm much taller than she is... (Crossing to BETTY in front of DELIA.) Well, Betty, what is it?

BETTY. The two gentlemen, Mr. Baxter and Mr. Devenish, have both called together, ma'am.

BELINDA (excited). Oh! How–how very simultaneous of them!

DELIA (eagerly, going towards house). Oh, do let me see them!

BELINDA (stopping her). Darling, you'll see plenty of them before you've finished. (To BETTY in an exaggerated whisper.) What have you done with them?

BETTY. They're waiting in the hall, ma'am, while I said I would see if you were at home.

BELINDA. All right, Betty. Give me two minutes and then show them out here.

BETTY. Yes, ma'am.

(BETTY crosses below BELINDA and DELIA and exits into the house.)

BELINDA (taking DELIA down R. a step). They can't do much harm to each other in two minutes.

DELIA (taking her hat from table). Well, I'll go and unpack. (She goes back to BELINDA.) You really won't mind my coming down afterwards?

BELINDA. Of course not. (A little awkwardly, taking DELIA'S arm and moving down R.) Darling one, I wonder if you'd mind–just at first–being introduced as my niece. (By now at foot of deck-chair.) You see, I expect they're in a bad temper already (now C.), having come here together, and we don't want to spoil their day entirely.

DELIA (smiling, on BELINDA'S L.). I'll be your mother if you like.

BELINDA. Oh no, that wouldn't do, because then Mr. Baxter would feel that he ought to ask your permission before paying his attentions to me. He's just that sort of man. A niece is so safe–however good you are at statistics, you can't really prove anything.

DELIA. All right, mummy.

BELINDA (enjoying herself). You'd like to be called by a different name, wouldn't you? There's something so thrilling about taking a false name. Such a lot of adventures begin like that. How would you like to be Miss Robinson, darling? It's a nice easy one to remember. (Persuasively.) And you shall put your hair up so as to feel more disguised. What fun we're going to have!

DELIA. You baby! All right, then, I'm Miss Robinson, your favourite niece. (She takes her jacket from the hammock and moves towards the house.)

BELINDA. How sweet of you! No, no, not that way–you'll meet them. (Following quickly up between tree and table to DELIA, who has now reached the house.) Oh, I'm coming with you to do your hair. (Moving up C., arm in arm with DELIA.) You don't think you're going to be allowed to do it yourself, when so much depends on it, and husbands leave you because of it, and—

(BELINDA, seeing BETTY entering from house, hurries DELIA up R., and they bob down behind the yew hedge R. BETTY comes from the house into the garden, crossing to centre and up stage looking for BELINDA, followed by MR. BAXTER and MR. DEVENISH. BAXTER gives an angry look round at DEVENISH as he enters. MR. BAXTER is forty-five, prim and erect, with close-trimmed moustache and side-whiskers. His clothes are dark and he wears a bowler-hat. MR. DEVENISH is a long-haired, good-looking boy in a négligé costume; perhaps twenty-two years old, and very scornful of the world. BAXTER crosses to L. below BETTY, and turns to her with a sharp inquiring glance. DEVENISH moves down R., languidly admiring the garden.)

  Belinda An April Folly In Three Acts

BETTY (looking about her surprised). The mistress was here a moment ago. (The two heads pop up from behind the hedge and then down again immediately. BELINDA and DELIA exeunt R.). I expect she'll be back directly, if you'll just wait.

(She goes back into the house.)

(BAXTER, crossing to R., meets DEVENISH who has moved up R. BAXTER is annoyed and with an impatient gesture comes down between the tree and the table to chair L. and sits. DEVENISH throws his felt hat on to the table and walks to the back of the hammock. He sees the review in the hammock and picks it up.)

DEVENISH. Good heavens, Baxter, she's been reading your article!

BAXTER. I dare say she's not the only one.

DEVENISH. That's only guesswork (going to back of table); you don't know of anyone else.

BAXTER (with contempt). How many people, may I ask, have bought your poems?

DEVENISH (loftily). I don't write for the mob.

BAXTER. I think I may say that of my own work.

DEVENISH. Baxter, I don't want to disappoint you, but I have reluctantly come to the conclusion that you are one of the mob. (Throws magazine down on table, annoyed.) Dash it! what are you doing in the country at all in a bowler-hat?

BAXTER. If I wanted to be personal, I could say, "Why don't you get your hair cut?" Only that form of schoolboy humour doesn't appeal to me.

DEVENISH. This is not a personal matter; I am protesting on behalf of nature. (Leaning against tree.) What do the birds and the flowers and the beautiful trees think of your hat?

BAXTER. If one began to ask oneself what the birds thought of things– (He pauses.)

DEVENISH. Well, and why shouldn't one ask oneself? It is better than asking oneself what the Stock Exchange thinks of things.

BAXTER. Well (looking up at DEVENISH'S extravagant hair), it's the nesting season. Your hair! (Suddenly.) Ha! ha! ha! ha! ha! ha!

DEVENISH (hastily smoothing it down). Really, Baxter, you're vulgar. (He turns away and resumes his promenading, going down R. and then round deck-chair to front of hammock. Suddenly he sees his book on the grass beneath the hammock and makes a dash for it.) Ha, my book! (Gloating over it.) Baxter, she reads my book.

BAXTER. I suppose you gave her a copy.

DEVENISH (exultingly). Yes, I gave her a copy. My next book will be hers and hers alone.

BAXTER. Then let me say that, in my opinion, you took a very great liberty.

DEVENISH. Liberty! And this from a man who is continually forcing his unwelcome statistics upon her.

BAXTER. At any rate, I flatter myself that there is no suggestion of impropriety in anything that I write.

DEVENISH. I'm not so sure about that, Baxter.

BAXTER. What do you mean, sir?

DEVENISH. Did you read The Times this month on the new reviews!

BAXTER. Well!

DEVENISH. Oh, nothing. It just said, "Mr. Baxter's statistics are extremely suggestive."

(BAXTER makes a gesture of annoyance.)

I haven't read them, so of course I don't know what you've been up to.

BAXTER (rising, turning away in disgust and crossing up L). Pah!

DEVENISH. Poor old Baxter! (Puts book of poems down on table and crosses below chair and gathers a daffodil from a large vase down R. and saying "Poor old Baxter!" ad lib. BAXTER moves round back of hammock and to R., collides with DEVENISH and much annoyed goes down between table and tree towards chair down L.) Baxter–(moving to and leaning against tree R.)

BAXTER (turning to DEVENISH crossly). I wish you wouldn't keep calling me "Baxter."

DEVENISH. Harold.

(BAXTER displays annoyance, and continues his walk to L.)

BAXTER. It is only by accident–an accident which we both deplore–that we have met at all, and in any case I am a considerably older man than yourself. (Sits L.)

DEVENISH. Mr. Baxter–father–(gesture of annoyance from BAXTER)–I have a proposal to make. We will leave it to this beautiful flower to decide which of us the lady loves.

BAXTER (turning round). Eh?

DEVENISH (pulling off the petals). She loves me, she loves Mr. Baxter, she loves me, she loves Mr. Baxter–(BELINDA appears in the porch)–Heaven help her!–she loves me—

BELINDA (coming down R.). What are you doing, Mr. Devenish!

DEVENISH (throwing away the flower and bowing very low). My lady.

(BAXTER rises quickly.)

BAXTER (removing his bowler-hat stiffly). Good afternoon, Mrs. Tremayne.

(She gives her left hand to DEVENISH, who kisses it, and her right to BAXTER, who shakes it.)

BELINDA. How nice of you both to come!

BAXTER. Mr. Devenish and I are inseparable–apparently.

BELINDA. You haven't told me what you were doing, Mr. Devenish. Was it (plucking an imaginary flower) "This year, next year?" or "Silk, satin–"

DEVENISH. My lady, it was even more romantic than that. I have the honour to announce to your ladyship that Mr. Baxter is to be a sailor. (Dances round imitating the hornpipe.)

BELINDA (to BAXTER). Doesn't he talk nonsense?

BAXTER. He'll grow out of it. I did.

BELINDA (moving down R. and then to centre towards hammock). Oh, I hope not. I love talking nonsense, and I'm ever so old. (As they both start forward to protest.) Now which one of you will say it first?

DEVENISH. You are as old as the stars and as young as the dawn.

BAXTER. You are ten years younger than I am.

BELINDA. What sweet things to say! I don't know which I like best.

DEVENISH. Where will my lady sit!

BELINDA (with an exaggerated curtsy). I will recline in the hammock, an it please thee, my lord—

(BAXTER goes to the right of the hammock, saying "Allow me." DEVENISH moves to the left of the hammock and holds it, takes up a cushion which BAXTER snatches from him and places in hammock again.)

—only it's rather awkward getting in, Mr. Baxter. Perhaps you'd both better look at the tulips for a moment.

BAXTER. Oh–ah–yes. (Crosses down R., turns his back to the hammock and examines the flowers.)

DEVENISH (leaning over her). If only—

BELINDA. You'd better not say anything, Mr. Devenlsh. Keep it for your next volume. (He turns away and examines flowers on L. She sits on hammock.) One, two, three–(throws her legs over)–that was better than last time. (They turn round to see her safely in the hammock. DEVENISH leans against the L. tree at her feet, and BAXTER draws the deck-chair from the right side of the table and turns it round towards her. He presses his hat more firmly on and sits down.) I wonder if either of you can guess what I've been reading this afternoon!

DEVENISH (looking at her lovingly). I know.

BELINDA (giving him a fleeting look). How did you know?

DEVENISH. Well, I—

BELINDA (to BAXTER). Yes, Mr. Baxter, it was your article I was reading. If you'd come five minutes earlier you'd have found me wrestling–I mean revelling in it.

BAXTER. I am very greatly honoured, Mrs. Tremayne. Ah–it seemed to me a very interesting curve showing the rise and fall of—

BELINDA. I hadn't got up to the curves. They are interesting, aren't they? They are really more in Mr. Devenish's line. (To DEVENISH.) Mr. Devenish, it was a great disappointment to me that all the poems in your book seemed to be written to somebody else.

DEVENISH. It was before I met you, lady. They were addressed to the goddess of my imagination. It is only in these last few weeks that I have discovered her.

BELINDA. And discovered she was dark and not fair.

DEVENISH. She will be dark in my next volume.

BELINDA. Oh, how nice of her!

BAXTER (kindly). You should write a real poem to Mrs. Tremayne.

BELINDA (excitedly). Oh do! "To Belinda." I don't know what rhymes, except cinder. You could say your heart was like a cinder–all burnt up.

DEVENISH (pained). Oh, my lady, I'm afraid that is a cockney rhyme.

BELINDA. How thrilling! I've never been to Hampstead Heath.

DEVENISH. "Belinda." It is far too beautiful to rhyme with anything but itself.

BELINDA. Fancy! But what about Tremayne? (Singing.) Oh, I am Mrs. Tremayne, and I don't want to marry again.

DEVENISH (protesting). My lady!

BAXTER (protesting). Belinda!

BELINDA (pointing excitedly to BAXTER). There, that's the first time he's called me Belinda! This naughty boy–(indicating DEVENISH)–is always doing it–by accident.

DEVENISH. Are you serious?

BELINDA. Not as a rule.

DEVENISH. You're not going to marry again?

BELINDA. Well, who could I marry?

DEVENISH and BAXTER (together). Me!

BELINDA (dropping her eyes modestly). But this is England.

BAXTER (rising and taking off his hat, which he places on table, and going up to BELINDA). Mrs. Tremayne, I claim the right of age–of my greater years–to speak first.

DEVENISH. Mrs. Tremayne, I—

BELINDA (kindly to DEVENISH). You can speak afterwards, Mr. Devenish. It's so awkward when you both speak together. (To BAXTER, giving encouragement.) Yes?

BAXTER (moving down a little and then returning to BELINDA). Mrs. Tremayne, I am a man of substantial position–(DEVENISH sniggers–to BAXTER'S great annoyance.) and perhaps I may say of some repute in serious circles.

(DEVENISH sniggers again.)

All that I have, whether of material or mental endowment, I lay at your feet, together with an admiration which I cannot readily put into words. As my wife I think you would be happy, and I feel that with you by my side I could achieve even greater things.

BELINDA. How sweet of you! But I ought to tell you that I'm no good at figures.

DEVENISH (protesting). My lady—

BELINDA. I don't mean what you mean, Mr. Devenish. You wait till it's your turn. (To BAXTER.) Yes?

BAXTER (very formally). I ask you to marry me, Belinda.

BELINDA (settling herself happily and closing her eyes). O-oh!... Now it's your turn, Mr. Devenish.

DEVENISH (excitedly). Money–thank Heaven, I have no money. Reputation–thank Heaven, I have no reputation.

(BAXTER, very annoyed, moves down and sits on deck-chair.)

What can I offer you? Dreams–nothing but dreams. Come with me and I will show you the world through my dreams. What can I give you? Youth, freedom, beauty—

BAXTER. Debts.

BELINDA (still with her eyes shut). You mustn't interrupt, Mr. Baxter.

DEVENISH (leaning across hammock). Belinda, marry me and I will open your eyes to the beauty of the world. Come to me!

BELINDA (happily). O-oh! You've got such different ways of putting things. How can I choose between you?

DEVENISH. Then you will marry one of us?

BELINDA. You know I really oughtn't to.

BAXTER. I don't see why not.

BELINDA. Well, there's just a little difficulty in the way.

DEVENISH. What is it? I will remove it. For you I could remove anything –yes, even Baxter. (He looks at BAXTER, who is sitting more solidly than ever in his chair.)

BELINDA. And anyhow I should have to choose between you.

DEVENISH (in a whisper), choose me.

BAXTER (stiffly). Mrs. Tremayne does not require any prompting. A fair field and let the best man win.

DEVENISH (going across to and slapping the astonished BAXTER on the back). Aye, let the best man win! Well spoken, Baxter. (BAXTER is very annoyed. To BELINDA and going back to her L.) Send us out into the world upon some knightly quest, lady, and let the victor be rewarded.

BAXTER. I—er—ought to say that I should be unable to go very far. I have an engagement to speak at Newcastle on the 21st.

DEVENISH. Baxter, I will take no unfair advantage of you. Let the beard of the Lord Mayor of Newcastle be the talisman that my lady demands; I am satisfied.

BAXTER. This sort of thing is entirely contrary to my usual mode of life, but I will not be outfaced by a mere boy. (Rising.) I am prepared. (Going to her.)

DEVENISH. Speak, lady.

BELINDA (speaking in a deep, mysterious voice). Gentlemen, ye put wild thoughts into my head. In sooth, I am minded to send ye forth upon a quest that is passing strange. Know ye that there is a maid journeyed hither, hight Robinson—whose—(in her natural voice) what's the old for aunt?

BAXTER (hopefully). Mother's sister.

BELINDA. You know, I think I shall have to explain this in ordinary language. You won't mind very much, will you, Mr. Devenish?

DEVENISH. It is the spirit of this which matters, not the language which clothes it.

BELINDA. Oh, I'm so glad you think so. Well, now about Miss Robinson. She's my niece and she's just come to stay with me, and—poor girl—she's lost her father. Absolutely lost him. He disappeared ever such a long time ago, and poor Miss Robinson—Delia—naturally wants to find him. Poor girl! she can't think where he is.

DEVENISH (nobly). I will find him.

BELINDA. Oh, thank you, Mr. Devenish; Miss Robinson would be so much obliged.

BAXTER. Yes–er–but what have we to go upon? Beyond the fact that his name is Robinson—

BELINDA. I shouldn't go on that too much. You see, he may easily have changed it by now. He was never very much of a Robinson. Nothing to do with Peter or any of those.

DEVENISH. I will find him.

BAXTER (with a look of annoyance at DEVENISH). Well, can you tell us what he's like?

BELINDA. Well, it's such a long time since I saw him. (Looking down modestly.) Of course, I was quite a girl then. The only thing I know for certain is that he has a mole on his left arm about here. (She indicates a spot just below the elbow. BAXTER examines it closely.)

DEVENISH (folding his arms and looking nobly upwards). I will find him.

BAXTER. I am bound to inform you, Mrs. Tremayne, that even a trained detective could not give you very much hope in such a case. However, I will keep a look-out for him, and, of course, if—

DEVENISH. Fear not, lady, I will find him.

BAXTER (annoyed). Yes, you keep on saying that, but what have you got to go on?

DEVENISH (grandly). Faith! The faith which moves mountains.

BELINDA. Yes, and this is only just one small mole-hill, Mr. Baxter.

BAXTER. Yes, but still—

BELINDA. S'sh! here is Miss Robinson.

(BAXTER takes up his hat and moves below the deck-chair to R. to meet DELIA.)

If Mr. Devenish will hold the hammock while I alight–we don't want an accident—

(DELIA comes out of the house.)

–I can introduce you. (He helps her to get out, holding the hammock.) Thank you. Delia darling (DELIA moves down R.) this is Mr. Baxter,–and Mr. Devenish. My niece, Miss Robinson—

(DELIA shakes hands with BAXTER and moves to C. below BELINDA and shakes hands with DEVENISH.)

DELIA. How do you do?

BELINDA. Miss Robinson has just come over from France. Man Dieu, quel pays!

BAXTER. I hope you had a good crossing, Miss Robinson.

DELIA. Oh, I never mind about the crossing. (Very slowly and shyly.) Aunt Belinda–(She stops and smiles.)

BELINDA. Yes, dear?

DELIA. I believe tea is almost ready. I want mine, and I'm sure Mr. Baxter's hungry. (He sniggers approvingly.) Mr. Devenish scorns food, I expect.

DEVENISH (hurt). Why do you say that?

DELIA. Aren't you a poet?

BELINDA. Yes, darling, but that doesn't prevent him eating. He'll be absolutely lyrical over Betty's sandwiches.

DEVENISH. You won't deny me that inspiration, I hope, Miss Robinson.

BELINDA (taking DELIA'S arm and moving with her to below deck-chair). Well, let's go and see what they're like.

(DELIA moves up R.C. to below the porch, accompanied by BAXTER on her R. and DEVENISH, who follows her on her L. They all move towards the porch.)

Mr. Baxter, just a moment.

BAXTER (apologizing to DELIA and moving in front of the others to back of deck-chair.) Yes?

(DELIA gathers a daffodil from a vase R. and places it in DEVENISH'S buttonhole.)

BELINDA (secretly). Not a word to her about Mr. Robinson. It must be a surprise for her.

BAXTER. Quite so, I understand.

BELINDA. That's right. (BAXTER rejoins DELIA. Raising her voice.) Oh, Mr. Devenish.

(DEVENISH, who is evidently much attracted by DELIA, apologizes to her and goes back between tree and hammock to L. of BELINDA.)

DEVENISH. Yes, Mrs. Tremayne?

BELINDA (secretly). Not a word to her about Mr. Robinson. It must be a surprise for her.

DEVENISH. Of course! I shouldn't dream–(Indignantly.) Robinson! What an unsuitable name!

(BAXTER and DELIA are just going into the house.)

BELINDA (dismissing DEVENISH). All right, I'll catch you up. (DEVENISH goes after the other two.)

(Left alone, BELINDA laughs happily to herself, and then begins to look rather aimlessly about her. She picks up her sunshade and opens it. She comes to the hammock, picks out her handkerchief, says, "Ah, there you are!" and puts it away. She goes slowly towards the house. TREMAYNE enters from L. and with his back to the audience tries latch of imaginary gate below scenic painted gateway L. BELINDA turns her head, hearing imaginary click of the garden gate L. She comes slowly back R.C.)

BELINDA (seeing TREMAYNE). Have you lost yourself, or something? No; the latch is this side. ... Yes, that's right.

(TREMAYNE comes in. He has been knocking about the world for eighteen years, and is very much a man, though he has kept his manners. His hair is greying a little at the sides, and he looks the forty-odd that he is. Without his moustache and beard he is very different from the boy BELINDA married.)

TREMAYNE (with his hat in his hand). I'm afraid I'm trespassing.

BELINDA (winningly, moving down R. a little). But it's such a pretty garden (turns away, dosing her parasol), isn't it?

(TREMAYNE, half recognizing her, moves to back of hammock and leans across to obtain a better view of her.)

TREMAYNE (rather confused). I-I beg your pardon, I-er— (He is wondering if it can possibly be she. BELINDA thinks his confusion is due to the fact that he is trespassing, and hastens to put him at his ease.)

BELINDA. I should have done the same myself, you know.

TREMAYNE (pulling himself together). Oh, but you mustn't think I just came in because I liked the garden—

BELINDA (clapping her hands). No; but say you do like it, quick.

TREMAYNE. It's lovely and— (He hesitates.)

BELINDA (hopefully). Yes?

TREMAYNE (with conviction). Yes, it's lovely. BELINDA (with that happy sigh of hers). O-oh! ... Now tell me what really did happen?

TREMAYNE. I was on my way to Marytown—

BELINDA. To where?

TREMAYNE. Marytown.

BELINDA. Oh, you mean Mariton.

TREMAYNE. Do I?

BELINDA. Yes; we always call it Mariton down here. (Earnestly.) You don't mind, do you?

TREMAYNE (smiling). Not a bit.

BELINDA. Just say it–to see if you've got it right.

TREMAYNE. Mariton.

BELINDA (shaking her head). Oh no, that's quite wrong. Try it again (With a rustic accent.) Mariton.

TREMAYNE. Mariton.

BELINDA. Yes, that's much better .... (As if it were he who had interrupted.) Well, do go on.

TREMAYNE. I'm afraid it isn't much of an apology really. I saw what looked like a private road (points L.), but what I rather hoped wasn't, and–well, I thought I'd risk it. I do hope you'll forgive me.

BELINDA. Oh, but I love people seeing my garden. Are you staying in Mariton?

TREMAYNE. I think so. Oh yes, decidedly.

BELINDA. Well, perhaps the next time the road won't feel so private.

TREMAYNE. How charming of you! (He feels he must know. A piano is heard off playing "Belinda." The tune is continued until the fall of the curtain.) Are you Mrs. Tremayne by any chance?

BELINDA. Yes.

TREMAYNE (nodding to himself). Yes.

BELINDA. How did you know?

TREMAYNE (hastily inventing, moving down L. below the hammock). They use you as a sign-post in the village. Past Mrs. Tremayne's house and then bear to the left—

BELINDA. And you couldn't go past it?

TREMAYNE. I'm afraid I couldn't. Thank you so much for not minding. (Going up to the L. of her.) Well, I must be getting on, I have trespassed quite enough.

BELINDA (regretfully). And you haven't really seen the garden yet.

TREMAYNE. If you won't mind my going on this way, I shall see some more on my way out.

BELINDA. Please do. It likes being looked at. (With the faintest suggestion of demureness.) All pretty things do.

TREMAYNE. Thank you very much. (Turns to go up c.) Er–(He hesitates.)

BELINDA (helpfully). Yes?

TREMAYNE. I wonder if you'd mind very much if I called one day to thank you formally for the lesson you gave me in pronunciation?

BELINDA (gravely). Yes. I almost think you ought to. I think it's the correct thing to do.

TREMAYNE (contentedly). Thank you very much, Mrs. Tremayne.

BELINDA. You'll come in quite formally (pointing to R. with her sunshade) by the front-door next time, won't you, because–because that seems the only chance of my getting to know your name.

TREMAYNE. Oh, I beg your pardon. My name is–er–er–Robinson.

(She is highly amused and looks round towards the house, recalling to her mind DELIA.)

BELINDA (laughing). How very odd!

TREMAYNE (startled). Odd?

BELINDA. Yes; we have some one called Robinson (nodding towards the house) staying in the house. I wonder if she is any relation?

TREMAYNE (hastily). Oh no, no. No, she couldn't be. I have no relations called Robinson–not to speak of.

BELINDA. You must tell me all about your relations when you come and call, Mr. Robinson.

TREMAYNE. I think we can find something better worth talking about than that.

BELINDA. Do you think so? (He says "Yes" with his eyes, bows, and moves up C. The piano is now forte. BELINDA accompanies him up a little, then stops. He turns in entrance up C., and they exchange glances. TREMAYNE exits to R., behind yew hedge. BELINDA stays looking after him, then moves down to back of table and picking up the book of poems, gives that happy sigh of hers, only even more so.) O-oh!

(Enter BETTY from porch.)

BETTY. If you please, ma'am, Miss Delia says, are you coming in to tea?

BELINDA (looking straight in front of her, and taking no notice of BETTY, in a happy, dreamy voice). Betty, ... about callers .... If Mr. Robinson calls—he's the handsome gentleman who hasn't been here before (puts book down)–you will say, "Not at home." And he will say, "Oh!" And you will say, "I beg your pardon, sir, was it Mr. Robinson?" And he will say, "Yes!" And you will say, "Oh, I beg your pardon, sir–" (Almost as if she were BETTY, she begins to move towards the house.) "This way–" (she would be smiling an invitation over her shoulder to MR. ROBINSON, if he were there, and she were BETTY)–"please!" (And the abandoned woman goes in to tea.)

Curtain

Act - II

It is morning in BELINDA'S hall, a low-roofed, oak-beamed place, comfortably furnished as a sitting-room. There is an inner and an outer front-door, both of which are open. Up C. is a door leading to a small room where hats and coats are kept. A door on the L. leads towards the living-rooms.

DEVENISH enters from up L. at back, passes the windows of the inner room and crosses to the porch. He rings the electric bell outside, then enters through the swing doors R.C. BETTY enters R. and moves up at back of settee R. to DEVENISH by the swing doors. He is carrying a large bunch of violets and adopts a very aesthetic attitude.

BETTY. Good morning, sir.

DEVENISH. Good morning. I am afraid this is an unceremonious hour for a call, but my sense of beauty urged me hither in defiance of convention.

BETTY. Yes, sir.

DEVENISH (holding up his bouquet to BETTY). See, the dew is yet lingering upon them; how could I let them wait until this afternoon?

BETTY. Yes, sir; but I think the mistress is out.

DEVENISH. They are not for your mistress; they are for Miss Delia.

BETTY. Oh, I beg your pardon, sir. If you will come in, I'll see if I can find her. (She crosses to the door R. and goes away to find DELIA, dosing the door after her.)

(DEVENISH tries a number of poses about the room for himself and hit bouquet. He crosses below the table C. and sits L. of it and is about to place his elbow on the table when he finds the toy dog which has been placed there is in his way. He removes it to the centre of the table and then leans with his elbow on table and finds this pose unsuitable so he crosses to above the fireplace and leans against the upper portico, resting on his elbow which slips and nearly prostrates him. He then crosses up to L. of the cupboard door at back centre and leans on his elbow against the wall.)

(Enter DELIA from the door R.)

DELIA (shutting the door and going to DEVENISH). Oh, good morning, Mr. Devenish.

[Illustration :]

(DEVENISH kisses her hand.)

I'm afraid my–er–aunt is out.

DEVENISH. I know, Miss Delia, I know.

DELIA. She'll be so sorry to have missed you. It is her day for you, isn't it?

DEVENISH. Her day for me?

DELIA. Yes; Mr. Baxter generally comes to-morrow, doesn't he?

DEVENISH (jealously). Miss Delia, if our friendship is to progress at all, it can only be on the distinct understanding that I take no interest whatever (coming to back of table C.) in Mr. Baxter's movements.

DELIA (moving down R. a little). Oh, I'm so sorry; I thought you knew. What lovely flowers! Are they for my aunt?

DEVENISH. To whom does one bring violets? To modest, shrinking, tender youth.

DELIA. I don't think we have anybody here like that.

DEVENISH (with a bow and holding out the violets to her). Miss Delia, they are for you.

DELIA (smelling and taking violets). Oh, how nice of you! But I'm afraid I oughtn't to take them from you under false pretences; I don't shrink.

DEVENISH. A fanciful way of putting it, perhaps. They are none the less for you.

DELIA. Well, it's awfully kind of you. (Puts flowers down. Then she moves up to the cupboard. He follows on her L. and opens the door.) I'm afraid I'm not a very romantic person. (Turning to him in cupboard doorway.) Aunt Belinda does all the romancing in our family.

DEVENISH. Your aunt is a very remarkable woman.

DELIA. She is. Don't you dare to say a word against her. (Takes up a vase from a chair in cupboard and shakes it as if draining it.)

DEVENISH. My dear Miss Delia, nothing could be further from my thoughts. Why, am I not indebted to her for that great happiness which has come to me in these last few days?

DELIA (surprised). Good gracious! and I didn't know anything about it. (Coming down to R. of table with vase.) But what about poor Mr. Baxter?

DEVENISH (stiffly, crossing over to fireplace, very annoyed). I must beg that Mr. Baxter's name be kept out of our conversation.

DELIA (going up to table behind Chesterfield up L.). But I thought Mr. Baxter and you were such friends.

(DELIA takes water carafe from the table and smiles at DEVENISH– which he does not see.)

Do tell me what's happened. (Moving down to R. of table C., she sits and arranges the flowers.) I seem to have lost myself.

DEVENISH (coming to the back of C. table and reclining on it.) What has happened, Miss Delia, is that I have learnt at last the secret that my heart has been striving to tell me for weeks past. As soon as I saw that gracious lady, your aunt, I knew that I was in love. Foolishly I took it for granted that it was she for whom my heart was thrilling. How mistaken I was! Directly you came, you opened my eyes, and now—

DELIA. Mr. Devenish, you don't say you're proposing to me?

DEVENISH. I am. I feel sure I am. (Leaning towards her.) Delia, I love you.

DELIA. How exciting of you!

DEVENISH (with a modest shrug). It's nothing; I am a poet.

DELIA. You really want to marry me?

DEVENISH. Such is my earnest wish.

DELIA. But what about my aunt?

DEVENISH (simply). She will be my aunt-in-law.

DELIA. She'll be rather surprised.

DEVENISH. Delia, I will be frank with you. (Sits.) I admit that I made Mrs. Tremayne an offer of marriage.

DELIA (excitedly). You really did? Was it that first afternoon I came?

DEVENISH. Yes.

DELIA. Oh, I wish I'd been there!

DEVENISH (with dignity, rising and moving to L. of table). It is not my custom to propose in the presence of a third party. It is true that on the occasion you mention a man called Baxter was on the lawn, but I regarded him no more than the old apple-tree or the flower-beds, or any other of the fixtures.

DELIA. What did she say?

DEVENISH. She accepted me conditionally.

DELIA. Oh, do tell me!

DEVENISH. It is rather an unhappy story. This man called Baxter in his vulgar way also made a proposal of marriage. Mrs. Tremayne was gracious enough to imply that she would marry whichever one of us fulfilled a certain condition.

DELIA. How sweet of her!

DEVENISH. It is my earnest hope, Miss Delia, that the man called Baxter will be the victor. As far as is consistent with honour, I shall endeavour to let Mr. Baxter (banging the table with his hand) win.

DELIA. What was the condition?

DEVENISH. That I am not at liberty to tell.

DELIA. Oh!

DEVENISH. It is, I understand, to be a surprise for you.

DELIA. How exciting! (Rising and taking vase of violets which she places up R.) Mr. Devenish, you have been very frank (coming to front of settee R. and sitting). May I be equally so?

(DEVENISH crosses to her and bows in acquiescence.) Why do you wear your hair so long?

DEVENISH (pleased). You have noticed it?

DELIA. Well, yes, I have.

DEVENISH. I wear it so to express my contempt for the conventions of so-called society. DELIA. I always thought that people wore it very very short if they despised the conventions of society.

DEVENISH. I think that the mere fact that my hair annoys Mr. Baxter is sufficient justification for its length.

DELIA. But if it annoys me too?

DEVENISH (heroically). It shall go. (Sits on settee above DELIA.)

(BELINDA enters from up L. with a garden basket supposed to contain cutlets. She crosses the windows at back.)

DELIA (apologetically). I told you I wasn't a very romantic person, didn't I? (Kindly.) You can always grow it again if you fall in love with somebody else.

DEVENISH. That is cruel of you, Delia. I shall never fall in love again.

(Enter BELINDA through swing doors B.C.)

BELINDA. Why, it's Mr. Devenish!

(DEVENISH rises and kisses her hand somewhat sheepishly.)

How nice of you to come so early in the morning! How is Mr. Baxter!

DEVENISH (annoyed and crossing behind BELINDA to her L.). I do not know, Mrs. Tremayne.

BELINDA (coming down to DELIA and sitting in the place vacated by DEVENISH). I got most of the things, Delia. (To DEVENISH.) "The things," Mr. Devenish, is my rather stuffy way of referring to all the delightful poems that you are going to eat to-night.

DEVENISH. I am looking forward to it immensely, Mrs. Tremayne.

BELINDA. I do hope I've got all your and Mr. Baxter's favourite dishes.

DEVENISH (annoyed and, moving to L. foot of table C.). I'm afraid Mr. Baxter and I are not likely to appreciate the same things.

BELINDA (coyly). Oh, Mr. Devenish! And you were so unanimous a few days ago.

DELIA. I think Mr. Devenish was referring entirely to things to eat.

BELINDA. I felt quite sad when I was buying the lamb cutlets. To think that, only a few days before, they had been frisking about with their mammas, and having poems written about them by Mr. Devenish. There! I'm giving away the whole dinner. Delia, take him away before I tell him any more.

(DELIA rises, goes to table and picks up water carafe which she replaces on refectory table up L.)

We must keep some surprises for him.

DELIA (to DEVENISH as she crosses back to table R. and picks up the flowers). Come along, Mr. Devenish.

BELINDA (wickedly). Are those my flowers, Mr. Devenish?

DEVENISH (advancing to BELINDA and laughing awkwardly, after a little hesitation, with a bow which might refer to either of them). They are for the most beautiful lady in the land.

BELINDA. Oh, how nice of you!

(DEVENISH crosses to door R. and opens it for DELIA, who follows him and exits. DEVENISH, standing above door, catches BELINDA'S eye and with an awkward laugh follows DELIA.)

BELINDA. I suppose he means Delia–bless them! (She kisses her hand towards the door R. She then rises and crosses below the table C., placing her basket on the L. end of it, to the fireplace. She rings the bell. Then she moves up on the R. side of the Chesterfield to the refectory table and takes off her hat. She takes up a mirror from the table and gives a few pats to her hair, and as she is doing so BETTY enters from door R. and crosses the room towards C.)

BELINDA (pointing to basket on the C. table). Oh, Betty—

(BETTY moves to back of C. table and takes up the basket. Crosses above settee and exits through door R. BELINDA is moving towards the swing doors when she catches sight of BAXTER entering from the garden up R. She moves quickly to the L. of C. table, takes up a book and going to Chesterfield L., lies down with her head to R. BAXTER looks in through the window up R., then crosses round and enters through the portico and the swing doors. BELINDA pretends to be very busy reading.)

BAXTER (rather nervously, in front of wring doors). Er–may I come in, Mrs. Tremayne?

BELINDA (dropping her book and turning round with a violent start). Oh, Mr. Baxter, how you surprised me! (She puts her hand to her heart and sits up and faces him.)

BAXTER. I must apologize for intruding upon you at this hour, Mrs. Tremayne.

BELINDA (holding up her hand). Stop!

BAXTER (startled). What?

BELINDA. I cannot let you come in like that.

BAXTER (looking down at himself). Like what?

BELINDA (dropping her eyes). You called me Belinda once.

BAXTER (coming down to her). May I explain my position, Mrs. Tremayne?

BELINDA. Before you begin–have you been seeing my niece lately?

BAXTER (surprised). No.

BELINDA. Oh! (Sweetly.) Please go on.

BAXTER. Why, is she lost too?

BELINDA. Oh no; I just— Do sit down.

(BAXTER moves to the chair L. of C. table and sits. BELINDA rises when he has sat down.)

Let me put your hat down somewhere for you.

BAXTER (keeping it firmly in his hand). It will be all right here, thank you.

BELINDA (returning to the Chesterfield and sitting). I'm dying to hear what you are going to say.

BAXTER. First as regards the use of your Christian name. I felt that, as a man of honour, I could not permit myself to use it until I had established my right over that of Mr. Devenish.

BELINDA. All my friends call me Belinda.

BAXTER. As between myself and Mr. Devenish the case is somewhat different. Until one of us is successful over the other in the quest upon which you have sent us, I feel that as far as possible we should hold aloof from you.

BELINDA (pleadingly). Just say "Belinda" once more, in case you're a long time.

BAXTER (very formally). Belinda.

BELINDA. How nicely you say it–Harold.

BAXTER (getting out of his seat). Mrs. Tremayne, I must not listen to this.

BELINDA (meekly). I won't offend again, Mr. Baxter. Please go on. (She motions him to sit–he does so.) Tell me about the quest; are you winning?

BAXTER. I am progressing, Mrs. Tremayne. Indeed, I came here this morning to acquaint you with the results of my investigations. (Clears his throat.) Yesterday I located a man called Robinson working upon a farm close by. I ventured to ask him if he had any marks upon him by which he could be recognized. He adopted a threatening attitude, and replied that if I wanted any he could give me some. With the aid of half-a-crown I managed to placate him. Putting my inquiry in another form, I asked if he had any moles. A regrettable misunderstanding, which led to a fruitless journey to another part of the village, was eventually cleared up, and on my return I satisfied myself that this man was in no way related to your niece.

BELINDA (admiringly). How splendid of you!

BAXTER. Yes.

BELINDA. Well, now, we know he's not. (She holds up one finger.)

BAXTER. Yes. In the afternoon I located another Mr. Robinson following the profession of a carrier. My first inquiries led to a similar result, with the exception that in this case Mr. Robinson carried his threatening attitude so far as to take off his coat and roll up his sleeves. Perceiving at once that he was not the man, I withdrew.

BELINDA. How brave you are!

BAXTER. Yes.

BELINDA. That makes two.

BAXTER. Yea.

BELINDA (holding up another finger). It still leaves a good many. (Pleadingly.) Just call me Belinda again.

BAXTER (rising and backing to R. a little, nervously). You mustn't tempt me, Mrs. Tremayne.

BELINDA (penitently). I won't!

BAXTER (going slowly to fireplace and placing his hat down on armchair below fireplace). To resume, then, my narrative. This morning I have heard of a third Mr. Robinson. Whether there is actually any particular fortune attached to the number three I cannot say for certain. It is doubtful whether statistics would be found to support the popular belief. But one likes to flatter oneself that in one's own case it may be true; and so—

BELINDA. And so the third Mr. Robinson–?

BAXTER. Something for which I cannot altogether account inspires me with hope. He is, I have discovered, staying at Mariton. This afternoon I go to look for him.

BELINDA (to herself). Mariton! How funny! I wonder if it's the same one.

BAXTER. What one?

BELINDA. Oh, just one of the ones. (Gratefully.) Mr. Baxter, you are doing all this for me.

BAXTER. Pray do not mention it. I don't know if it's Devonshire (going to and sitting L. of BELINDA), or the time of the year, or the sort of atmosphere you create, Mrs. Tremayne, but I feel an entirely different man. There is something in the air which–yes, I shall certainly go over to Mariton this afternoon.

BELINDA (gravely). I have had the same feeling sometimes, Mr. Baxter. I am not always the staid respectable matron which I appear to you to be. Sometimes I–(She looks absently at the watch on her wrist.) Good gracious!

BAXTER (alarmed). What is it!

BELINDA (looking anxiously from the door to him). Mr. Baxter, I'm going to throw myself on your mercy.

BAXTER. My dear Mrs. Tremayne—

BELINDA (looking at her watch again, rising and moving up L.C., looking at door). A strange man will be here directly. He must not find you with me.

BAXTER (rising, jealously). A man?

BELINDA (excitedly). Yes, yes, a man! He is pursuing me with his attentions. If he found you here, there would be a terrible scene.

BAXTER. I will defend you from him.

BELINDA (crossing down to R. of Chesterfield). No, no. He is a big man. He will–he will overpower you. (Moving L. a little and looking out of windows.)

BAXTER. But you–!

BELINDA. I can defend myself. I will send him away. But he must not find you here. You must hide before he overpowers you.

BAXTER (with dignity, crossing below table to R.). I will withdraw if you wish it. BELINDA (following to R. at back of table C.). No, not withdraw, hide. He might see you withdrawing. (Leading the way to the cupboard door.) Quick, in here.

BAXTER (embarrassed at the thought that this sort of thing really only happens in a bedroom farce and moving towards her). I don't think I quite—

BELINDA (reassuring him). It's perfectly respectable; it's where we keep the umbrellas. (She takes him by the hand.)

BAXTER (resisting and looking nervously into the cupboard). I'm not at all sure that I—

BELINDA (earnestly). Oh, but don't you see what trust I'm putting in you? (To herself.) Some people are so nervous about their umbrellas.

BAXTER. Well, of course, if you–but I don't see why I shouldn't just slip out of the door before he comes.

BELINDA (reproachfully). Of course, if you grudge me every little pleasure–(Crossing in front of BAXTER towards swing doors and seeing TREMAYNE coming.) Quick! Here he is.

(She bundles him through the cupboard door and closes it and with a sign of happiness crosses down to C. table. She sees BAXTER'S bowler hat on the arm-chair below the fireplace. She fetches and carries it over to the cupboard door, knocks and hands it to him, saying, "Your hat!")

BAXTER (expostulating and nearly knocking her over as he comes out). Well, really I—

BELINDA (bundling him into the cupboard and closing the door). Hush!

(BELINDA straightens her hair, takes up her book from L. of C. table and sits, stroking the head of the toy dog and pretending to read. TREMAYNE enters from garden up R. and through the swing doors up R.C.. BELINDA gives an assumed cry of surprise.)

TREMAYNE (at the swing doors). It's no good your pretending to be surprised, because you said I could come. (Coming down to the back of the table C. and putting down his hat.)

BELINDA (rising, shaking hands and welcoming him). But I can still be surprised that you wanted to come.

TREMAYNE Oh no, you aren't.

BELINDA (marking it off on her fingers). Just a little bit–that much.

TREMAYNE. It would be much more surprising if I hadn't come.

BELINDA (crossing to the Chesterfield, picking up her book and handing it to TREMAYNE, who puts it on the table). It is a pretty garden, isn't it? (She sits on R. end of Chesterfield.)

TREMAYNE (coming to her). You forget that I saw the garden yesterday.

BELINDA. Oh, but the things have grown so much since then. Let me see, this is the third day you've been and we only met three days ago. (He moves behind the Chesterfield to the left end of it.) And then you're coming to dinner again to-night.

TREMAYNE (eagerly and leaning over the Chesterfield). Am I?

BELINDA. Yes. Haven't you been asked?

TREMAYNE (going round the left end of the Chesterfield). No, not a word.

BELINDA. Yes, that's quite right; I remember now, I only thought of it this morning, so I couldn't ask you before, could I?

TREMAYNE (earnestly). What made you think of it then?

BELINDA (romantically). It was at the butcher's.

TREMAYNE. Eh?

BELINDA. There was one little lamb cutlet left over and sitting out all by itself, and there was nobody to love it. And I said to myself, suddenly, "I know, that will do for Mr. Robinson." (Protaically.) I do hope you like lamb?

TREMAYNE (sitting on her left side). I adore it.

BELINDA. Oh, I'm so glad I When I saw it sitting there I thought you'd love it. I'm afraid I can't tell you any more about the rest of the dinner, because I wouldn't tell Mr. Devenish, and I want to be fair.

TREMAYNE (jealously). Who's Mr. Devenish?

BELINDA. Oh, haven't you met him? He's always coming here.

TREMAYNE Is he in love with you too?

BELINDA. Too? Oh, you mean Mr. Baxter?

TREMAYNE (rising and moving to fireplace). Confound it, that's three!

BELINDA (innocently). Three? (She looks up at him and down again.)

TREMAYNE. Who is Mr. Baxter?

BELINDA. Oh, haven't you met him? He's always coming here.

TREMAYNE (turning away and looking into fireplace). Who is Mr. Baxter?

(BAXTER appears at cupboard doorway. BELINDA hears him and gives a startled look round. She signs to him to go back. BAXTER retreats immediately and closes door.)

BELINDA. Oh, he's a sort of statistician. Isn't that a horrid word to say? So stishany.

TREMAYNE. What does he make statistics about?

BELINDA. Oh (giving a sly look round at cupboard door), umbrellas and things. Don't let's talk about him.

TREMAYNE. All right, then; (going up to her jealously) who is Mr. Devenish?

BELINDA. Oh, he's a poet. (She throws up her eyes and sighs deeply.) Ah me!

TREMAYNE. What does he write poetry about?

(BELINDA looks at him, and down again, and then at him again, and then down, then raises and drops her arms, and gives a little sigh–all of which means, "Can't you guess?")

What does he write poetry about?

BELINDA (obediently). He wrote "The Lute of Love and other Poems, by Claude Devenish."

(TREMAYNE is annoyed and turns away to the fireplace.)

The Lute of Love–(To herself.) I haven't been saying that lately. (With great expression.) The Lute of Love–the Lute. (She pats her mouth back.)

TREMAYNE. And who is Mr. Devenish–!

BELINDA (putting her hand on his sleeve). You'll let me know when it's my turn, won't you?

TREMAYNE. Your turn?

BELINDA. Yes, to ask questions. I love this game–it's just like clumps. (She crosses her hands on her lap and waits for the next question.)

TREMAYNE. I beg your pardon. I–er–of course have no right to cross-examine you like this.

BELINDA. Oh, do go on, I love it. (With childish excitement.) I've got my question ready.

TREMAYNE (smiling and going and sitting beside her again). I think perhaps it is your turn.

BELINDA (eagerly). Is it really? (He nods.) Well then–(in a loud voice)–who is Mr. Robinson?

TREMAYNE (alarmed). What?

BELINDA. I think it's a fair question. I met you three days ago and you told me you were staying at Mariton. Mariton. You can say it all right now, can't you?

TREMAYNE. I think so.

BELINDA (coaxingly). Just say it.

TREMAYNE. Mariton.

BELINDA (clapping her hands). Lovely! I don't think any of the villagers do it as well as that.

TREMAYNE. Well?

BELINDA (looking very hard at TREMAYNE–he wonders whether she has discovered his identity). Well, that was three days ago. You came the next day to see the garden, and you came the day after to see the garden, and you've come this morning–to see the garden; and you're coming to dinner to-night, and it's so lovely, we shall simply have to go into the garden afterwards. And all I know about you is that you haven't any relations called Robinson.

TREMAYNE. What do I know about Mrs. Tremayne but that she has a relation called Robinson?

BELINDA. And two dear friends called Devenish and Baxter.

TREMAYNE (rising–annoyed). I was forgetting them. (Crosses to below L. end of C. table.)

BELINDA (to herself, with a sly look round at the cupboard), I mustn't forget Mr. Baxter.

TREMAYNE. But what does it matter? What would it matter if I knew nothing about you? (Moving up to R. end of Chesterfield and leaning over it.) I know everything about you–everything that matters.

BELINDA (leaning back and closing her eyes contentedly). Tell me some of them. TREMAYNE (bending over her earnestly). Belinda—

BELINDA (still with her eyes shut). He's going to propose to me. I can feel it coming.

TREMAYNE (starting back). Confound it! how many men have proposed to you?

BELINDA (surprised). Since when?

TREMAYNE. Since your first husband proposed to you.

BELINDA. Oh, I thought you meant this year. (Sitting up.) Well now, let me see. (Slowly and thoughtfully.) One. (She pushes up her first finger.) Two. (She pushes up the second.) Three. (She pushes up the third finger, holds it there for a moment and then pushes it gently down again.) No, I don't think that one ought to count really. (She pushes up two more fingers and the thumb.) Three, four, five–do you want the names or just the total?

TREMAYNE (moving up L. and then over R.). This is horrible.

BELINDA (innocently). But anybody can propose. Now if you'd asked how many I'd accepted—

(He turns sharply to her–annoyed.)

Let me see, where was I up to?

(He moves down R.)

I shan't count yours, because I haven't really had it yet.

(BETTY enters down R. and stands behind settee.)

Six, seven–Yes, Betty, what is it?

BETTY. If you please, ma'am, cook would like to speak to you for a minute.

(TREMAYNE goes up R.C.)

BELINDA (getting up). Yes, I'll come.

(BETTY goes out, leaving the door open. BELINDA crosses Before the table.)

(To TREMAYNE.) You'll forgive me, won't you? You'll find some cigarettes there. (Points to table up R. TREMAYNE moves by the back of the settee and holds the door for BELINDA. She turns to him in the doorway.) It's probably about the lamb cutlets; I expect your little one refuses to be cooked.

(She goes out after BETTY.)

(Left alone TREMAYNE stalks moodily about the room, crossing it and kicking things which come in his way. Violently, he kicks a hassock which is above the table R. to under the table C., then he takes up his hat and moves towards the swing doors and half opens them. He pauses and considers– then he comes down to the centre table, throws down his hat, moves round the left end of the table, finds the dog in the way and then sits on the table with his hands in his pockets, facing the audience. As he has been moving about the room, he has muttered the names of BAXTER and DEVENISH.)

DEVENISH (entering from the door R., which he closes and goes to foot of the settee R.–surprised). Hullo!

(A pause.)

TREMAYNE (jealously, and rising). Are you Mr. Devenish?

DEVENISH. Yes.

TREMAYNE. Devenish the poet?

DEVENISH (coming up and shaking him warmly by the hand). My dear fellow, you know my work?

TREMAYNE (grimly). My dear Mr. Devenish, your name is most familiar to me.

DEVENISH. I congratulate you. I thought your great-grand-children would be the first to hear of me.

TREMAYNE (moving to L.). My name's Robinson, by the way.

DEVENISH (connecting him with DELIA). Then let me return the compliment, Robinson. Your name is familiar to me.

TREMAYNE (hastily, and going towards DEVENISH). I don't think I'm related to any Robinsons you know.

DEVENISH (dubiously). Well, no, I suppose not. When I was very much younger I began a collection of Robinsons. Actually it was only three days ago, but it seems much longer. (Thinking of DELIA.) Many things have happened since then.

TREMAYNE (uninterested, moving L.) Really!

DEVENISH. There is a man called Baxter–(TREMAYNE displays his jealousy of BAXTER.) who is still collecting, I believe. For myself, I am only interested in one of the great family–Delia.

TREMAYNE (eagerly, and going quickly to him and placing his hand on DEVENISH'S left shoulder). You are interested in her?

DEVENISH. Devotedly. In fact, I am at this moment waiting for her to put on her hat.

TREMAYNE (warmly, banging him on the shoulder with both hands). My dear Devenish, I am delighted to make your acquaintance. (He seizes his hand and grips it heartily.) How are you? (DEVENISH backs to the settee in pain.)

DEVENISH (sitting on settee, feeling his fingers). Fairly well, thanks.

TREMAYNE (sitting above him and banging him on the back). That's right.

DEVENISH (still nursing his hand). You are a very lucky fellow, Robinson.

TREMAYNE. In what way?

DEVENISH. People you meet must be so very reluctant to say good-bye to you. Have you ever tried strangling lions or anything like that?

TREMAYNE (with a laugh). Well, as a matter of fact, I have.

DEVENISH. I suppose you won all right?

TREMAYNE. In the end, with the help of my beater.

DEVENISH. Personally I should have backed you alone against any two ordinary lions.

TREMAYNE. One was quite enough. As it was, he gave me something to remember him by. (Putting up his left sleeve, he displays a deep scar.)

DEVENISH (looking at it casually). By Jove, that's a nasty one! (He suddenly catches sight of the mole and stares at it fascinated, then stares up at TREMAYNE.) Good heavens!

TREMAYNE. What's the matter?

DEVENISH (clasping his head). Wait. (Rising and moving up to L. of TREMAYNE.) Let me think. (After a pause.) Have you ever met a man called Baxter?

TREMAYNE. No.

DEVENISH. Would you like to?

TREMAYNE (grimly). Very much indeed.

DEVENISH. He's the man I told you about who's interested in Robinsons. He'll be delighted to meet you. (With a nervous laugh.) Funny thing, he's rather an authority on lions. You must show him that scar of yours; it will intrigue him immensely. (Earnestly.) Don't shake hands with him too heartily just at first; it might put him off the whole thing.

TREMAYNE. This Mr. Baxter seems to be a curious man.

DEVENISH (absently). Yes, he is rather odd. (Looking at his watch.) I wonder if I–(To TREMAYNE.) I suppose you won't be— (He stops suddenly. A slight tapping noise comes from the room where they keep umbrellas.)

TREMAYNE. What's that!

(The tapping noise is repeated, a little more loudly this time. DEVENISH moves to end of table.)

DEVENISH. Come in.

(The door opens and BAXTER comes in nervously, holding his bowler hat in his hand. He moves towards the swing doors.)

BAXTER (apologetically). Oh, I just–(TREMAYNE stands up) –I just–(He goes back again.)

DEVENISH (springing across the room). Baxter!

(The door opens nervously again and BAXTER'S head appears round it.)

Come in, Baxter, old man; you're just the very person I wanted.

(BAXTER comes in carefully. DEVENISH closes the door.)

Good man. (To TREMAYNE, taking BAXTER down R., and placing his arm round his shoulders.) This is Mr. Baxter that I was telling you about.

(BAXTER removes DEVENISH'S arm from his shoulders.)

TREMAYNE (moving up to BAXTER and much relieved at the appearance of his rival). Oh, is this Mr. Baxter? (Holding out his hand with great friendliness.) How are you, Mr. Baxter?

DEVENISH (warningly). Steady!

(TREMAYNE shakes BAXTER quite gently by the hand.)

Baxter, this is Mr. Robinson. (Casually.) R-o-b-i-n-s-o-n. (He looks sideways at BAXTER to see how he takes it. BAXTER is noticeably impressed.)

BAXTER. Really? I am very glad to meet you, sir.

TREMAYNE. Very good of you to say so.

DEVENISH (to BAXTER, taking his arm. BAXTER is annoyed and gets free). Robinson is a great big-game hunter.

BAXTER (moving down to TREMAYNE). Indeed? I have never done anything in that way myself, but I'm sure it must be an absorbing pursuit.

TREMAYNE. Oh, well, it's something to do.

DEVENISH (to BAXTER). You must get him to tell you about a wrestle he had with a lion once. Extraordinary story! (Looking at his watch suddenly.) Jove! I must be off. See you again, Baxter. (He bangs BAXTER on the shoulder and moves down to TREMAYNE.) Good-bye, Robinson. No, don't shake hands. I'm in a hurry. (He looks at his watch again and goes out hurriedly by the door on the R.)

(TREMAYNE sits on settee R. and BAXTER on chair R. of C. table. He puts his hat on the table.)

TREMAYNE. Unusual man, your friend Devenish. I suppose it comes of being a poet.

BAXTER. I have no great liking for Mr. Devenish—

TREMAYNE. Oh, he's all right.

BAXTER. But I am sure that if he is impressed by anything outside himself or his own works, it must be something rather remarkable. Pray tell me of your adventure with the lion.

TREMAYNE (laughing). Really, you mustn't think that I go about telling everybody my adventures. It just happened to come up. I'm afraid I shook his hand rather more warmly than I meant, and he asked me if I'd ever tried strangling lions. That was all.

BAXTER. And had you?

TREMAYNE. Well, it just happened that I had.

BAXTER. Indeed! You came off scatheless, I trust?

TREMAYNE (carelessly indicating his arm). Well, he got me one across there.

BAXTER (rising and coming to above TREMAYNE, obviously excited). Really, really. (Points to his arm.) One across there. Not bad, I hope?

.TREMAYNE (laughing). Well, it doesn't show unless I do that. (He pulls up his sleeve carelessly and BAXTER bends eagerly over his arm and sees the mole and very slowly looks up at TREMAYNE, then down at the arm again, then up at TREMAYNE.)

BAXTER. Good heavens! I've found it! (He runs over to the table and picks up his hat.)

TREMAYNE. Found what? (He pulls down his sleeve.)

BAXTER (going up L.). I must see Mrs. Tremayne. Where's Mrs. Tremayne?

TREMAYNE. She went out just now. What's the matter?

BAXTER. Out! I must find her. This is a matter of life and death. (He hurries through the swing doors.) Mrs. Tremayne! Mrs. Tremayne! (He exits R. through the garden.)

(TREMAYNE rises and moves to the swing doors, stares after him in amazement. Then he pulls up his sleeve, looks at his scar again and shakes his head. While he is still puzzling over it, BELINDA comes back R.)

BELINDA (crossing below settee). Such a to-do in the kitchen! The cook's given notice–at least she will directly–(up to TREMAYNE)–and your lamb cutlet slipped back to the shop when nobody was looking

(TREMAYNE looks off at swing doors)

and I've got to go into the village again, (going to the refectory table and getting her hat) and ok dear, oh dear, I have such a lot of things to do! (Looking across at MR. BAXTER'S door.) Oh yes, that's another one. (Coming back to table C. and putting down her hat on R. side.)

TREMAYNE. Belinda— (Moving up to her.)

BELINDA. No, not even Belinda. Wait till this evening.

TREMAYNE. I have a thousand things to say to you; I shall say them this evening.

BELINDA (giving him her hand). Begin about eight o'clock. Good-bye till then.

(He takes her hand, looks at her for a moment, then suddenly bends and kisses it, takes up his hat and hurries through the swing doors and off through the garden to L.)

(BELINDA stands looking from her hand to him, gives a little wondering exclamation and then presses the back of her hand against her cheek, and goes to the swing doors. She turns back, and remembers MR. BAXTER again. With a smile she goes to the door and taps gently.)

BELINDA. Mr. Baxter, Mr. Baxter, you may come in now; he has withdrawn. (Moves down a little and then back to L. of the door again.) Mr. Baxter, I have unhanded him. (She opens the door and going in, finds the room empty.) Oh!

(BAXTER comes quickly through the swing doors.)

BAXTER (meeting BELINDA coming out of the cupboard). Ah, (they both start) there you are! (Crossing down to R. end of C. table, he puts down his hat.)

BELINDA (turning with a start). Oh, how you frightened me, Mr. Baxter! I couldn't think what had happened to you. (She closes the door.) I thought perhaps you'd been eaten up by one of the umbrellas.

BAXTER. Mrs. Tremayne, I have some wonderful news for you. I have found Miss Robinson's father.

BELINDA (on his L., hardly understanding). Miss Robinson's father?

BAXTER. Yes. Mr. Robinson.

BELINDA. Oh, you mean–(Points to direction when TREMAYNE has gone.) Oh yes, he told me his name was Robinson–Oh, but he's no relation.

BAXTER. Wait! I saw his arm. By a subterfuge I managed to see his arm.

BELINDA (her eyes opening more and more widely as she begins to realize). You saw—

BAXTER. I saw the mole.

BELINDA (coming down to him faintly as she holds out her own arm). Show me.

BAXTER (very decorously indicating). There!

(BELINDA holds the place with her other hand, and still looking at MR. BAXTER, slowly begins to laugh–half-laughter, half-tears, wonderingly, happily, contentedly.)

BELINDA (moving to R. of table and sitting). And I didn't know!

BAXTER (moving to back of table). Mrs. Tremayne, I am delighted to have done this service for your niece—

BELINDA (to herself). Of course, he knew all the time.

BAXTER (to the world). Still more am I delighted to have gained the victory over Mr. Devenish in this enterprise.

BELINDA. Eighteen years–but I ought to have known.

BAXTER (at large). I shall not be accused of exaggerating when I say that the odds against such an enterprise were enormous.

BELINDA. Eighteen years— And now I've eight whole hours to wait!

BAXTER (triumphantly). It will be announced to-night. "Mr. Devenish," I shall say, "young fellow–" (He arranges his speech in his mind.)

BELINDA (nodding to herself mischievously). So I was right, after all! (Slowly and triumphantly.) He does look better without a beard!

BAXTER (with his hand on the back of the chair on the L. side of the table). "Mr. Devenish, young fellow, when you matched yourself against a man of my repute, when you matched yourself against a man–matched yourself against a man of my repute (crossing towards fireplace)

(BELINDA rises stealthily, takes up her hat and exits through the swing doors and through the garden up R.)

when you matched yourself against a man who has read papers (moving towards centre table) at Soirees of the Royal Statistical Society–" (Looking round the room, he discovers that he is alone. He picks up his hat from the table and jams it down on his head.) Unusual!

(He moves up towards the swing doors.)

Curtain.

Act - III

It is after dinner in BELINDA'S hall. The log fire, chandelier and wall brackets are all alight. BELINDA is lying on the Chesterfield with a coffee-cup in her hand. DELIA, in the chair down L. below the fireplace, has picked up "The Lute of Love" from a table and is reading it impatiently. She also has a coffee-cup in her hand.

DELIA (throwing the book away). What rubbish he writes!

BELINDA (coming back from her thoughts). Who, dear?

DELIA. Claude

(BELINDA gives her a quick look of surprise.)

–Mr. Devenish. (She rises and stands by the fireplace with her cup in her hand.) Of course, he's very young.

BELINDA. So was Keats, darling.

DELIA. I don't think Claude has had Keats' advantages. Keats started life as an apothecary.

BELINDA. So much nicer than a chemist.

DELIA. Now, Claude started with nothing to do.

BELINDA (mildly). Do you always call him Claude, darling? I hope you aren't going to grow into a flirt like that horrid Mrs. Tremayne.

DELIA. Silly mother! (She moves to BELINDA, takes her cup, then crosses to the table and places both the cups on the table–seriously.) I don't think he'll ever be any good till he really gets work. Did you notice his hair this evening?

BELINDA (dreamily). Whose, dear?

DELIA (going to the back of the Chesterfield and to the L. of BELINDA). Mummy, look me in the eye and tell me you are not being bad.

BELINDA (having playfully turned her head away and hidden her face with her handkerchief, says innocently). Bad, darling?

DELIA (moving down to the front of the fireplace). You've made Mr. Robinson fall in love with you.

BELINDA (happily). Have I?

DELIA. Yes; it's serious this time. He's not like the other two.

BELINDA. However did you know that?

DELIA. Oh, I know.

BELINDA. Darling, I believe you've grown up. It's quite time I settled down.

DELIA. With Mr. Robinson?

(BELINDA sits up and looks thoughtfully at DELIA for a little time.)

BELINDA (mysteriously). Delia, are you prepared for a great secret to be revealed to you?

DELIA (childishly and jumping on to the L. arm of the Chesterfield facing BELINDA). Oh, I love secrets.

BELINDA (reproachfully). Darling, you mustn't take it like that. This is a great, deep, dark secret; you'll probably need your sal volatile.

DELIA (excitedly). Go on!

BELINDA. Well— (Looking round the room.) Shall we have the lights down a little?

DELIA. Go on, mummy.

BELINDA. Well, Mr. Robinson is–(impressively)–is not quite the Robinson he appears to be.

DELIA. Yes?

BELINDA. In fact, child, he is— Darling, hadn't you better come and hold your mother's hand?

DELIA (struggling with some emotion and placing her hand on BELINDA'S arm, who playfully smacks it). Go on.

BELINDA. Well, Mr. Robinson is a–sort of relation of yours; in fact–(playing with her rings and looking down coyly)–he is your–father. (She looks up at DELIA to see how the news is being received.) (DELIA gives a happy laugh.)

Dear one, this is not a matter for mirth.

DELIA. Darling, it is lovely, isn't it? (Sliding down to the seat of the Chesterfield next to BELINDA, who moves along to make room for her.) I am laughing because I am so happy.

BELINDA. Aren't you surprised?

DELIA. No. You see, Claude told me this morning. (BELINDA displays annoyance.) He found out just before Mr. Baxter.

BELINDA. Well! Every one seems to have known except me.

DELIA. Didn't you see how friendly father and I got at dinner? I thought I'd better start breaking the ice–because I suppose he'll be kissing me directly.

BELINDA. Say you like him.

DELIA. I think he's going to be awfully nice. (She kisses BELINDA and rises.) Does he know you know?

BELINDA. Not yet.

DELIA. Oh! (She moves to the fireplace and warms her hands.)

BELINDA. Just at present I've rather got Mr. Baxter on my mind. I suppose, darling, you wouldn't like him as well as Mr. Devenish! (Pathetically.) You see, they're so used to going about together.

DELIA. Claude is quite enough.

BELINDA. I think I must see Mr. Baxter and get it over. Do you mind if I have Mr. Devenish too? I feel more at home with both of them. I'll give you him back. Oh dear, I feel so happy to-night! (She jumps up and goes to DELIA.) And is my little girl going to be happy too? That's what mothers always say on the stage. I think it's so sweet.

(They move together to below table.)

DELIA (smiling at her). Yes, I think so, mummy. Of course, I'm not romantic like you. I expect I'm more like father, really.

BELINDA (dreamily). Jack can be romantic now. He was telling me this morning all about the people he has proposed to. I mean, I was telling him. Anyhow, he wasn't a bit like a father. Of course, he doesn't know he is a father yet. Darling, I think you might take him into the garden; only don't let him know who he is. You see, he ought to propose to me first, oughtn't he?

(The men come in from R. TREMAYNE goes to the foot of the settee R., DEVENISH to the back of the table up R., while BAXTER stands at the back of the settee. BELINDA moves to the front of the settee and DELIA sits on the table.)

Here you all are! I do hope you haven't been throwing away your cigars, because smoking is allowed all over the house.

TREMAYNE (as he comes to the foot of the settee). Oh, we've finished, thank you.

BELINDA (going up to the swing doors and opening them). Isn't it a wonderful night?–and so warm for April. Delia, you must show Mr. Robinson the garden by moonlight–it's the only light he hasn't seen it by.

DEVENISH (quickly coming to R. back of table C.). I don't think I've ever seen it by moonlight, Miss Delia.

BELINDA (coming down a little). I thought poets were always seeing things by moonlight.

BAXTER (moving toward BELINDA). I was hoping, Mrs. Tremayne, that–er–perhaps—

DELIA (moving quickly to above TREMAYNE and taking his L. hand, and pulling him up stage to swing doors). Come along, Mr. Robinson.

(TREMAYNE looks at BELINDA, who gives him a nod. BELINDA then moves down R.)

TREMAYNE (L. of DELIA). It's very kind of you, Miss Robinson. I suppose there is no chance of a nightingale?

BELINDA. There ought to be. I ordered one specially for Mr. Devenish.

(DELIA and TREMAYNE go out together. BELINDA, with a sigh, moves over to the Chesterfield and settles herself comfortably into it. DEVENISH, annoyed by TREMAYNE'S attentions to DELIA, crosses up angrily and looks off through the window up L. above fireplace, then comes down L. of the Chesterfield to the front of the fireplace. BAXTER moves up to the swing doors angrily watching DELIA and TREMAYNE, then moves to the window R. and looks off. BETTY then enters with a salver from R. She moves by the back of the settee to the back of the table C., picks up the coffee-cups and goes out R. BAXTER then moves over to the window facing the audience, up L. He looks off, then comes down to the R. of BELINDA.)

Now we're together again. Well, Mr. Devenish?

DEVENISH. Er–I—

BELINDA. No; I think I'll let Mr. Baxter speak first. I know he's longing to.

BAXTER (leaning on the back of the chair L. of table–he clears his throat). H'r'm! Mrs. Tremayne, I beg formally to claim your hand.

BELINDA (sweetly). On what grounds, Mr. Baxter?

DEVENISH (spiritedly). Yes, sir, on what grounds?

BAXTER (coming to R. of Chesterfield, close to BELINDA). On the grounds that, as I told you this morning, I had succeeded in the quest.

DEVENISH (appearing to be greatly surprised). Succeeded?

BAXTER. Yes, Mr. Devenish, young fellow, you have lost. (He moves a few paces R. to below the chair L. of the table.) I have discovered the missing Mr. Robinson.

DEVENISH (wiping hit brow and coming to BAXTER). Who–where—

BAXTER (dramatically). Miss Robinson has at this moment gone out with her father.

DEVENISH (placing his hands heavily on BAXTER'S shoulders, who staggers). Good heavens! It was he!

(BAXTER pats DEVENISH sympathetically and moves to the back of the Chesterfield and is about to speak to BELINDA. She, however, silences him and he drops down to the front of the fireplace.)

BELINDA (sympathetically). Poor Mr. Devenish!

DEVENISH (pointing tragically to the table). And to think that I actually sat on that table–no, that seat (he points to the settee R., then he moves up stage between it and the table)–that I sat there with him this morning, and never guessed! Why, ten minutes ago I was asking him for the nuts!

BAXTER. Aha, Devenish, you're not so clever as you thought you were.

DEVENISH (coming quickly to the back of the chair L. of the table). Why, I must have given you the clue myself! He told me he had a scar on his arm, and I never thought any more of it. And then I went away innocently and left you two talking about it.

BELINDA (alarmed). A scar on his arm?

DEVENISH. Where a lion mauled him.

(BELINDA gives a little cry and shudder.)

BAXTER. It's quite healed up now, Mrs. Tremayne.

BELINDA (looking at him admiringly). A lion! What you two have adventured for my sake!

BAXTER. I suppose you will admit, Devenish, that I may fairly claim to have won?

(Looking the picture of despair, DEVENISH drops down L. of the chair, droops his head, raises his arms and lets them fall hopelessly to his sides.)

BELINDA. Mr. Devenish, I have never admired you so much as I do at this moment. (She extends her R. hand to DEVENISH, who gropes for it with his L. hand and eventually manages to seize it.)

BAXTER (noticing he is holding her hand, moving to them and looking at them quizzically–indignantly to DEVENISH). I say, you know, that's not fair. It's all very well to take your defeat like a man, but you mustn't overdo it. (They release their hands.) Mrs. Tremayne, I claim the reward which I have earned.

BELINDA (after a pause and rising). Mr. Baxter–Mr. Devenish, I have something to tell you.

(DEVENISH moves to her R.)

(BELINDA kneels upon the Chesterfield facing them. Penitently.) I have not been quite frank with you. I think you both ought to know that–I–I made a mistake. Delia is not my niece; she is my daughter. (She buries her face in her hands.)

DEVENISH. Your daughter! I say, how ripping!

(BELINDA gives him an understanding look.)

BAXTER. Your daughter!

BELINDA. Yes.

BAXTER. But–but you aren't old enough to have a daughter of that age.

BELINDA (apologetically). Well, there she is.

BAXTER. But–but she's grown up.

BELINDA. Quite.

BAXTER. Then in that case you must be–(He hesitates, evidently working it out.)

BELINDA (hastily). I'm afraid so, Mr. Baxter.

BAXTER. But this makes a great difference. I had no idea. Why, when I'm fifty you would be—

BELINDA (sighing). Yes, I suppose I should.

BAXTER. And when I'm sixty—

BELINDA (pleadingly to DEVENISH). Can't you stop him?

DEVENISH (with a threatening gesture). Look here, Baxter, another word from you and you'll never get to sixty.

BAXTER. And then there's Miss–er–Delia. In the event of our marrying, Mrs. Tremayne, she, I take it, would be my step-daughter.

BELINDA. I don't think she would trouble us much, Mr. Baxter. (With a sly look at DEVENISH.) I have an idea that she will be getting married before long. (She again glances at DEVENISH, who returns her look gratefully.)

BAXTER (moving up L. into the inner room). None the less, the fact would be disturbing.

(DEVENISH with a wink at BELINDA crosses in front of her and warms his hands at the fire. BELINDA watches BAXTER over the back of the Chesterfield.)

I have never yet considered myself seriously as a step-father. (Moving round the refectory table.) I don't think I am going too far if I say that to some extent I have been deceived in this matter. (He comes down to behind the C. table.)

BELINDA (reproachfully). And so have I. I thought you loved me.

DEVENISH (sympathetically). Yes, yes.

BELINDA (turning to him suddenly). And Mr. Devenish too.

BAXTER (moving to BELINDA). Er—

DEVENISH. Er—

(They stand before her guiltily and have nothing to say.)

BELINDA (with a shrug). Well, I shall have to marry somebody else, that's all.

BAXTER (moving to below table). Who? Who?

BELINDA. I suppose Mr. Robinson. After all, if I am Delia's mother, and Mr. Baxter says that Mr. Robinson's her father, it's about time we were married.

DEVENISH (eagerly). Mrs. Tremayne, what fools we are! He is your husband all the time!

BELINDA. Yes.

BAXTER (moving up to the R. of BELINDA). You've had a husband all the time?

BELINDA (apologetically). I lost him; it wasn't my fault.

BAXTER. Really, this is very confusing. I don't know where I am. I gather–I am to gather, it seems, that you are no longer eligible as a possible wife?

BELINDA. I am afraid not, Mr. Baxter.

BAXTER. But this is very confusing–(moving towards the swing doors)–this is very disturbing to a man of my age. For weeks past I have been regarding myself as a–a possible benedict. I have–ah–taken steps. (Back to the L. end of the C. table.) Only this morning, in writing to my housekeeper, I warned her that she might hear at any moment a most startling announcement.

DEVENISH (cheerfully). Oh, that's all right. That might only mean that you were getting a new bowler-hat.

BAXTER (dropping down L.C. a few steps–suddenly). Ah, and what about you, sir? How is it that you take this so lightly? (Triumphantly.) I have it. It all becomes clear to me. You have transferred your affections to her daughter!

DEVENISH. Oh, I say, Baxter, this is very crude.

BELINDA. And why should he not, Mr. Baxter? (Softly.) He has made me very happy.

BAXTER (staggered). He has made you happy, Mrs. Tremayne!

BELINDA. Very happy.

BAXTER (thoughtfully). Oh! Oh ho! Oh ho! (He takes a turn up the room into the inner room, muttering to himself. BELINDA kneels and watches him over the back of the Chesterfield. Then he comes down again to her R. side.) Mrs. Tremayne, I have taken a great resolve. (Solemnly.) I also will make you happy. (Thumping his heart.) I also will woo Miss Delia.

BELINDA. Oh!

DEVENISH. Look here, Baxter—

BAXTER (suddenly crossing and seizing DEVENISH'S arm and pulling him towards the siding doors up R. between the Chesterfield and the table). Come, we will seek Miss Delia together.

(BELINDA seizes DEVENISH'S hand as he is passing and he, clinging to it, nearly pulls her off the Chesterfield. She is very amused.)

It may be that she will send us upon another quest in which I shall again be victorious.

(BELINDA releases her hand and slips down into the Chesterfield. Tempestuously.)

Come, I say—

(He marches the resisting DEVENISH to the swing doors.)

Let us put it to the touch, to win or lose it all.

DEVENISH (turning and appealing to BELINDA). Please!

BELINDA (gently). Mr. Baxter... Harold.

(BAXTER stops and turns round.)

You are too impetuous. I think that as Delia's mother—

BAXTER (coming down R. to the foot of the C. table). Your pardon, Mrs. Tremayne. In the intoxication of the moment I am forgetting. (Formally.) I have the honour to ask your permission to pay my addresses–(Moves to chair L. of table.)

BELINDA. No, no, I didn't mean that. But, as Delia's mother, I ought to warn you that she is hardly fitted to take the place of your housekeeper. She is not very domesticated.

BAXTER (indignantly). Not domesticated? (Sits L. of table.) Why, did I not hear her tell her father at dinner that she had arranged all the flowers?

BELINDA. There are other things than flowers.

DEVENISH (on BAXTER'S R., behind the table). Bed-socks, for instance, Baxter.

(BAXTER is annoyed.)

It's a very tricky thing airing bed-socks. I am sure your house-keeper—

BAXTER (silencing DEVENISH). Mrs. Tremayne, she will learn. The daughter of such a mother... I need say no more.

BELINDA. Oh, thank you. But there is something else, Mr. Baxter. You are not being quite fair to yourself. In starting out upon this simultaneous wooing, you forget that Mr. Devenish has already had his turn–(DEVENISH tries to stop her. BAXTER turns round and nearly catches him.)–this morning alone. You should have yours ... alone ... too.

DEVENISH. Oh, I say!

BAXTER. Yes, yes, you are right. I must introduce myself first as a suitor. I see that. (Rising, to DEVENISH.) You stay here; I will go alone into the garden, and–(Moving below table and up to the swing doors.)

BELINDA. It is perhaps a little cold out of doors for people of ... of our age, Mr. Baxter. Now, in the library—

BAXTER (at the swing doors, turning to her, astonished). Library?

BELINDA. Yes.

BAXTER (moving down R. a little). You have a library?

BELINDA (to DEVENISH). He doesn't believe I have a library.

DEVENISH. You ought to see the library, Baxter.

BAXTER (moving more down to below R. of table). But you are continually springing surprises on me this evening, Mrs. Tremayne. First a daughter, then a husband, and then–a library! I have been here three weeks, and I never knew you had a library. Dear me, I wonder how it is that I never saw it?

BELINDA (modestly, rising). I thought you came to see me.

BAXTER. Yes, yes, to see you, certainly. But if I had known you had a library ....

BELINDA. Oh, I am so glad I mentioned it. Wasn't it lucky, Mr. Devenish?

BAXTER. My work has been greatly handicapped of late.

(DELIA and TREMAYNE enter the garden from up L. and pass the window at the back.)

BELINDA (sweetly). By me?

BAXTER. I was about to say by lack of certain books to which I wanted to refer. It would be a great help. (He moves up R, reflectively muttering "Library.")

BELINDA (moving below and to R. of C. table). My dear Mr. Baxter, my whole library is at your disposal. (She turns to DEVENISH, who is on her L., and at the back of the table. She speaks in a confidential whisper.) I'm just going to show him the Encyclopedia Britannica. (She moves below the settee to the door R.) You won't mind waiting–Delia will be in directly.

(BAXTER, still muttering "Library," crosses to the door and opens it for her. She goes out and he follows her. DEVENISH moves to the R. of the swing doors and welcomes DELIA and TREMAYNE. TREMAYNE enters from the portico and holds open the swing doors for DELIA.)

DELIA (speaking from the portico). Hullo, we're just coming in.

(They enter and DELIA moves down R. of the table.)

TREMAYNE. Where's Mrs. Tremayne?

DEVENISH (moving to down R.). She's gone to the library with Baxter.

TREMAYNE (coming down on DELIA'S R. side–carelessly). Oh, the library. Where's that?

DEVENISH (promptly going towards the door, opening it and standing above it). The end door on the right.

(DELIA sits on the R. end of the table facing R.)

Right at the end. You can't mistake it. On the right.

TREMAYNE. Ah, yes. (He looks round at DELIA, who points significantly at the door twice.) Yes. (He looks at DEVENISH.) Yes. (He goes out.)

(DEVENISH hastily shuts the door and comes back to DELIA.)

DEVENISH. I say, your mother is a ripper.

DELIA (enthusiastically). Isn't she! (Remembering.) At least, you mean my aunt?

DEVENISH (smiling at her). No, I mean your mother. To think that I once had the cheek to propose to her.

DELIA. Oh! Is it cheek to propose to people!

DEVENISH. To her.

DELIA. But not to me?

DEVENISH. Oh I say, Delia!

DELIA (with great dignity). Thank you, my name is Miss Robinson–I mean, Tremayne.

DEVENISH. Well, if you're not quite sure which it is, it's much safer to call you Delia.

DELIA (smiling). Well, perhaps it is.

DEVENISH. And if I did propose to you, you haven't answered

DELIA (sitting in the chair R. of the table). If you want an answer now, it's no; but if you like to wait till next April—

DEVENISH (moving up to behind table–reproachfully). Oh, I say, and I cut my hair for you the same afternoon. (Turning quickly.) You haven't really told me how you like it yet.

DELIA. Oh, how bad of me! You look lovely.

DEVENISH (sitting at back of the table). And I promised to give up poetry for your sake.

DELIA. Perhaps I oughtn't to have asked you that.

DEVENISH. As far as I'm concerned, Delia, I'll do it gladly, but, of course, one has to think about posterity.

DELIA. But you needn't be a poet. You could give posterity plenty to think about if you were a statesman.

DEVENISH. I don't quite see your objection to poetry.

DELIA. You would be about the house so much. I want you to go away every day and do great things, and then come home in the evening and tell me all about it.

DEVENISH. Then you are thinking of marrying me!

DELIA. Well, I was just thinking in case I had to.

DEVENISH (he rises and taking her hands, raises her from the chair. She backs a step to R.). Do. It would be rather fun if you did. And look here–(he pulls her gently back. They both sit on the table. He places his arm round her waist)–I will be a statesman, if you like, and go up to Downing Street every day, and come back in the evening and tell you all about it.

DELIA. How nice of you!

DEVENISH (magnificently, holding up his L. hand to Heaven). Farewell, Parnassus!

DELIA (pulling down his hand). What does that mean?

DEVENISH. Well, it means that I've chucked poetry. A statesman's life is the life for me; behold Mr. Devenish, the new M.P.–(she holds up her L. hand admonishingly and he laughs apologetically)–no, look here, that was quite accidental.

DELIA (smiling at him). I believe I shall really like you when I get to know you.

DEVENISH. I don't know if it's you, or Devonshire, or the fact that I've had my hair cut, but I feel quite a different being from what I was three days ago.

DELIA. You are different. (They both rise from the table. She pulls him to R. one step.) Perhaps it's your sense of humour coming back.

DEVENISH. Perhaps that's it. It's a curious feeling.

DELIA (pulling him towards the swing doors). Let's go outside; there's a heavenly moon.

DEVENISH. Moon? Moon? Now where have I heard that word before?

DELIA. What do you mean?

DEVENISH. I was trying not to be a poet.

(DELIA opens the doors.)

Well, I'll come with you, but I shall refuse to look at it. (Putting his L. hand behind his back, he walks slowly out with her, saying to himself) The Prime Minister then left the House.

(They cross the windows at the back and go off L.)

(BELINDA and TREMAYNE come from the library, the latter holding the door for her to pass.)

BELINDA (moving below the settee across the room). Thank you. I don't think it's unkind to leave him, do you? He seemed quite happy.

TREMAYNE (following her). I shouldn't have been happy if we'd stayed.

BELINDA (reaching the Chesterfield she puts her feet up. Her head it towards L.). Yes, but I was really thinking of Mr. Baxter.

TREMAYNE (above table C.). Not of me?

BELINDA. Well, I thought it was Mr. Baxter's turn. Poor man, he's had a disappointment lately.

TREMAYNE (coming to R. of the Chesterfield–eagerly). A disappointment?

BELINDA. Yes, he thought I was–younger than I was.

TREMAYNE (smiling to himself). How old are you, Belinda?

BELINDA (dropping her eyes). Twenty-two. (After a pause.) He thought I was eighteen. Such a disappointment!

TREMAYNE (smiling openly at her). Belinda, how old are you?

BELINDA. Just about the right age, Mr. Robinson.

TREMAYNE. The right age for what?

BELINDA. For this sort of conversation.

TREMAYNE. Shall I tell you how old you are?

BELINDA. Do you mean in figures or–poetically?

TREMAYNE. I meant—

BELINDA. Mr. Devenish said I was as old as the–now, I must get this the right way round–as old as the—

TREMAYNE. I don't want to talk about Mr. Devenish.

BELINDA (with a sigh). Nobody ever does–except Mr. Devenish. As old as the stars, and as young as the dawn. (Settling herself cosily.) I think that's rather a nice age to be, don't you?

TREMAYNE. A very nice age to be.

BELINDA. It's a pity he's thrown me over for Delia; I shall miss that sort of thing rather. You don't say those sort of things about your aunt-in-law–not so often.

TREMAYNE (eagerly). He really is in love with Miss Robinson!

BELINDA. Oh yes. I expect he is out in the moonlight with her now, comparing her to Diana.

TREMAYNE. Well, that accounts for him. Now what about Baxter?

BELINDA. I thought I told you. Deeply disappointed to find that I was four years older than he expected, Mr. Baxter hurried from the drawing-room and buried himself in a column of the Encyclopedia Britannica.

TREMAYNE. Well, that settles Baxter. Are there any more men in the neighbourhood?

BELINDA (shaking her head). Isn't it awful? I've only had those two for the last three weeks.

(TREMAYNE sits on the back of the Chesterfield and looks down at her.)

TREMAYNE. Belinda.

BELINDA. Yes, Henry!

TREMAYNE. My name is John.

BELINDA. Well, you never told me. I had to guess. Everybody thinks they can call me Belinda without giving me the least idea what their own names are. You were saying, John?

TREMAYNE. My friends call me Jack.

BELINDA. Jack Robinson. That's the man who always goes away so quickly. I hope you're making more of a stay?

TREMAYNE (seizing her by both arms). Oh, you maddening, maddening woman!

BELINDA. Well, I have to keep the conversation going. You do nothing but say "Belinda."

TREMAYNE (taking her hand). Have you ever loved anybody seriously, Belinda?

BELINDA. I don't ever do anything very seriously. The late Mr. Tremayne, my first husband–Jack— Isn't it funny, his name was Jack–he used to complain about it too sometimes.

TREMAYNE (with conviction). Silly ass!

BELINDA. Ah, I think you are a little hard on the late Mr. Tremayne.

TREMAYNE. Belinda, I want you to marry me and forget about him.

BELINDA (happily to herself and lying back). This is the proposal that those lamb cutlets interrupted this morning.

TREMAYNE. Belinda, I love you–do you understand?

BELINDA. Suppose my first husband turns up suddenly like–like E. A.?

TREMAYNE. Like who?

BELINDA. Well, like anybody.

TREMAYNE. He won't–I know he won't. Don't you love me enough to risk it, Belinda?

BELINDA. I haven't really said I love you at all yet.

TREMAYNE. Well, say it now.

(BELINDA looks at him, and then down again.)

You do! Well, I'm going to have a kiss, anyway, (He kisses her quickly–moves to L. of Chesterfield.) There!

BELINDA (rising). O-oh I The late Mr. Tremayne never did that. (She powders her nose.)

TREMAYNE. I have already told you that he was a silly ass. (He makes a move as if to kiss her again.)

BELINDA (holding up her hand and sitting on the R. side of the Chesterfield). I shall scream for Mr. Baxter.

TREMAYNE (sitting down on the Chesterfield, on her L, side.) Belinda—

BELINDA. Yes, Henry–I mean, Jack?

TREMAYNE. Do you know who I am! (He is thoroughly enjoying the surprise he is about to give her.)

BELINDA (nodding). Yes, Jack.

TREMAYNE. Who?

BELINDA. Jack Tremayne.

TREMAYNE (jumping up). Good heavens, you know!

BELINDA (gently). Yes, Jack.

TREMAYNE (angrily). You've known all the time that I was your husband, and you've been playing with me and leading me on.

BELINDA (mildly). Well, darling, you knew all the time that I was your wife, and you've been making love to me and leading me on.

TREMAYNE. That's different.

BELINDA (to herself). That's just what the late Mr. Tremayne said, and then he slammed the door and went straight off to the Rocky Mountains and shot bears; and I didn't see him again for eighteen years.

TREMAYNE (remorsefully). Darling, I was a fool then, and I'm a fool now.

BELINDA. I was a fool then, but I'm not such a fool now–I'm not going to let you go. It's quite time I married and settled down.

TREMAYNE. You darling I (He kisses her.) How did you find out who I was?

BELINDA (awkwardly). Well, it was rather curious, darling. (After a pause.) It was April, and I felt all sort of Aprily, and–and–there was the garden all full of daffodils–and–and there was Mr. Baxter–the one we left in the library–knowing all about moles. He's probably got the M. volume down now. Well, we were talking about them one day, and I happened to say that the late Mr. Tremayne–that was you, darling–had rather a peculiar one on his arm. And then he happened to see it this morning and told me about it.

TREMAYNE. What an extraordinary story!

BELINDA. Yes, darling; it's really much more extraordinary than that. I think perhaps I'd better tell you the rest of it another time. (Coaxingly.) Now show me where the nasty lion scratched you.

(TREMAYNE pulls up his sleeve.) Oh! (She kisses his arm.) You shouldn't have left Chelsea, darling.

TREMAYNE. I should never have found you if I hadn't.

BELINDA (squeezing his arm). No, Jack, you wouldn't. (After a pause.) I–I've got another little surprise for you if–if you're ready for it. (Standing up and moving to the chair L. of the table.) Properly speaking, I ought to be wearing white. I shall certainly stand up while I'm telling you. (Modestly.) Darling, we have a daughter–our little Delia. (He is standing in front of the fireplace.)

TREMAYNE. Delia? You said her name was Robinson.

BELINDA. Yes, darling, but you said yours was. One always takes one's father's name. Unless, of course, you were Lord Robinson.

TREMAYNE. But you said her name was Robinson before you—

(She makes a playful move.)

–Oh, never mind about that. A daughter? Belinda, how could you let me go and not tell me?

BELINDA. You forget how you'd slammed the door. It isn't the sort of thing you shout through the window to a man on his way to America.

TREMAYNE (taking her in his arms). Oh, Belinda, don't let me ever go away again.

(DEVENISH and DELIA enter from up L. and pass the windows on the way to the swing doors.)

BELINDA. I'm not going to, Jack. I'm going to settle down into a staid old married woman.

TREMAYNE. Oh no, you're not. You're going on just as you did before. And I'm going to propose to you every April, and win you, over all the other men in love with you.

BELINDA. You darling! (They embrace.)

(DELIA and DEVENISH come in from the garden.)

TREMAYNE (quietly to BELINDA). Our daughter.

DELIA (going up to TREMAYNE). You're my father.

TREMAYNE. If you don't mind very much, Delia.

DELIA. You've been away a long time.

TREMAYNE. I'll do my best to make up for it.

BELINDA. Delia, darling, I think you might kiss your poor old father.

(As the does to, DEVENISH suddenly and hastily kisses BELINDA on the cheek.)

DEVENISH. Just in case you're going to be my mother-in-law.

TREMAYNE. We seem to be rather a family party.

BELINDA (suddenly). There! (Moving to the door L.) We've forgotten Mr. Baxter again.

BAXTER (who has come in quietly with a book in his hand). Oh, don't mind about me, Mrs. Tremayne. I've enjoyed myself immensely. (He crosses to the arm-chair below the fireplace and places it in front of the fire.)

(BELINDA and TREMAYNE move up into the inner room by the refectory table and embrace, their backs to BAXTER. DELIA and DEVENISH are by the swing doors. They also embrace, their backs to BAXTER.)

(Referring to his book.) I have been collecting some most valuable information on (looking round at them and sitting in the arm-chair and continuing to read) lunacy in the–er–county of Devonshire.

(The CURTAIN falls.)

THE END

9 789355 841988